Home Warming Holidays © Cookbook

From
The Kindred Cottage
Where Kindred Friends Share Kindred Thoughts

Filled With
**Recipes, Helpful Hints
Warm Thoughts**
And

The Home Warming
Block of the Month Quilt
Patterns and Instructions

Copyright 2000, Pearl Louise Krush
All rights reserved. No part of this book
may be reproduced in any form without permission of the
author. The patterns, instructions and designs are intended
for the retail purchaser and are under the federal copyright laws.
Projects may not be manufactured for commercial use.

In Appreciation

I would like to thank my family and wonderful customers
who have shared their favorite recipes and warm thoughts.
To my staff members Virginia Lowary for her recipes
and to Christine Bump for the quilt block drawings

To Julie Weaver, my executive assistant
who worked ever so diligently
on this book with me.
A Very Special THANK YOU !

ISBN: 0-942249-17-8
Library of Congress: 00-131552
First Printing, April 2000

Cover photograph by Starr-Toof
Cover design by Pearl Louise Designs

Published by
Toof Cookbook Division
STARR-TOOF
670 South Cooper Street
Memphis, Tennessee 38104
800-722-4772

Home Warming Holidays ©

New Year's Day .. New Beginnings Brunch 7
  Shivers Snowman Block of the Month 13

Valentine's Day .. Valentine Tea 17
  Angel of My Heart Block of the Month 22

St. Patrick's Day .. Saint Pat's Pot Luck 25
  Bird and Kite Block of the Month 31

Easter .. Bunny Buffet. 35
  Rainy Day & Tulips Block of the Month 41

Mother's Day .. Love You Lunch. 45
  Mother's Day Basket Block of the Month 51

Father's Day .. Delectables for Dad 55
  Gone Fishin' Block of the Month 61

Fourth of July .. Patriotic Party. 65
  Liberty Flag Block of the Month 71

August .. Fun In the Sun 75
  Sunflowers and Crow Block of the Month 81

Labor Day .. Leisure Time Lunch 85
  Back to School Block of the Month .91

Halloween .. A Ghoulish Good Time 95
  Pumpkin Surprise Block of the Month 101

Thanksgiving .. Oh Thankful Hearts 105
  Thomas P. Turkey Block of the Month 111

Christmas .. A Festive Feast 115
  Santa on His Way Block of the Month 121
  Home Warming Block of the Month Quilt 125

General Information:

All of the blocks used in the Block of the Month Quilt and other projects in this book are Double Star Blocks. Choose light, medium and dark fabrics to make your blocks. Block Building Instructions are on Page 16.

General Instructions:
Pre-wash and press fabrics. Use 1/4" seams throughout.
Press all seams toward the darkest color.

Fabrics Needed for each Block:
Star Points- 1/4 yd. Dark
Background- 1/3 yd. Medium
Center Block - 1/4 yd. Light
(See page 126 for materials needed to make the entire quilt.)

Applique Materials Needed and Instructions:
Scrap Fabrics and Iron On Fusible Web
The appliques used on all of the blocks are Iron On Fusible Web Appliques. Follow the instructions on the Iron On Fusible Web product you are using. Cut all patterns as stated and be aware of reversing the direction of the pieces if necessary. Add 1/4" to each applique should you choose to do the needle turn applique method.

Home Warming Holidays

Block of the Month Quilt

Block of the Month

Stitching Instructions:

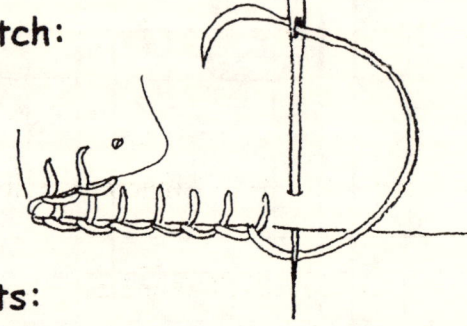

Blanket Stitch:

French Knots:

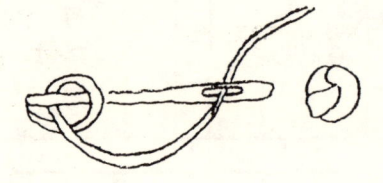

Chain Stitch:

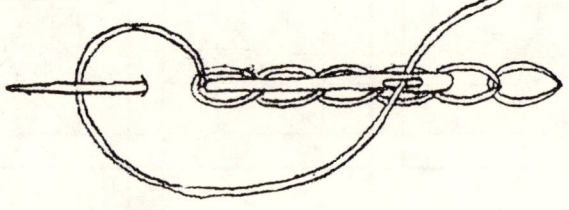

Lazy Daisy Stitch:

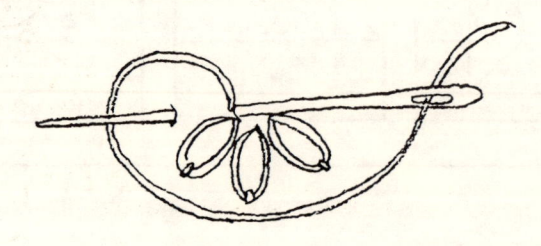

New Year's Day

New Beginnings Brunch Menu

Quick As A Wink Cinnamon Rolls

Fruity Crunch Salad

Eggs Extravaganza

Easy Breakfast Bake

Sparkling Orange Juice

Snowball Cookies

January Hints
And
Shivers Snowman
Block of the Month Pattern

Quick as a Wink Cinnamon Rolls

Rolls:
4 cups flour
3 tbsp. baking powder
4 tbsp. sugar
1 tsp. cream of tartar
1 tsp. salt

Cinnamon Topping:
3/4 cup butter or
 margarine (melted)
1 1/2 cups sugar
1/4 cup cinnamon

1 cup butter or margarine
1 1/3 cup milk
2 eggs (unbeaten)

Creamy Frosting:
3/4 cup butter or
 margarine (melted)
1 tbsp. vanilla
3 cups powdered sugar
milk

Preheat oven to 425°. Sift dry ingredients together. Cut softened butter or margarine into the flour mixture. Pour milk in slowly. Add the eggs. Stir until you have a stiff dough. Knead a few times and roll the dough into a 1/2" thickness. Spread the melted butter or margarine over the dough evenly. Mix the cinnamon and sugar together. Sprinkle the cinnamon mixture over the melted butter. Roll dough like a jelly roll. Cut dough into 1 1/2" inch pieces. Place the pieces on a greased cookie sheet. Bake 10 to 15 minutes or until the tops are slightly brown. While the rolls are baking, mix vanilla, melted butter or margarine together with the powdered sugar. Pour only enough milk into the frosting until the frosting is easy to spread. Spread the frosting onto each roll and serve while warm.

Cut cinnamon rolls or other rolls or cookies into slices by using thread or dental floss. Simply slide the thread or floss under the roll of dough, bring the thread ends up. Cross the thread or floss and pull. Cut perfect slices every time!!!

Butter Twist Coffee Cake

4 cups flour
4 tbsp. sugar
1 tsp. salt
1/2 cup butter or margarine
3 eggs

1 can evaporated milk (5.3 oz.)
2 tbsp. water
1 ounce cake yeast
1/4 cup warm water
2 tsp. sugar

Mix dry ingredients together with margarine. Scald and cool the milk and 2 tbsp. water. Add yeast, softened in 1/4 cup warm water, eggs and 2 tsp. sugar to milk mixture. Mix wet and dry ingredients together until the dough leaves the sides of the bowl. Grease another bowl and place the dough in the greased bowl. Refrigerate overnight. Divide the dough into six parts. Roll each section into a 10" long roll. Twist two together and place in a crescent shape on greased 9" pans. Let rise 1/2 hour. Bake 30 minutes at 350°. Frost with orange icing while warm.

Orange Icing

1 package cream cheese, softened (8 oz.)
1/2 cup margarine or butter, softened
1/4 cup orange juice

3 tbsp. grated orange peel
2 tsp. vanilla
3 cups powdered sugar

Mix cheese and margarine or butter together. Add the orange juice, orange peel and vanilla. Mix thoroughly. Stir in powdered sugar until smooth. Drizzle over the coffee cake while warm.

*Gather together the simple joys of life.
Scatter them throughout the year.*

Snowball Cookies

1/2 cup crunchy peanut butter
1/4 cup butter or margarine, softened
1 cup chopped walnuts
1 1/2 cup Rice Krispies

Icing:
1 cup powdered sugar
3 tbsp. milk
1/2 tsp. vanilla
flaked coconut

Cream together peanut butter, butter or margarine and sugar. Add walnuts and Rice Krispies. Mix well. Form into 1" balls and refrigerate for 1/2 hour.

Icing:
Mix powdered sugar, milk and vanilla. Roll balls in frosting and then in coconut. Makes 2 dozen cookies.

Make New Year's resolutions that are easy to break. You won't have the GUILT!

Make time for yourself! Put on your favorite music, turn off the lights, light a scented candle and get in a warm bubble bath.

Start your deep cleaning in January. Do one room at a time and you will be done in time to enjoy the outdoors come Spring!!!

Fruity Crunch Salad

2 apples, unpeeled
1/2 cup walnuts
2 stalks celery
1/2 cup raisins

2 oranges, peeled
1/2 cup orange juice
3 tbsp. honey

Chop apples, walnuts, celery and peeled oranges. Stir the fruits and nuts together. Mix the orange juice, lemon juice and honey. Pour over fruit and nut mixture. Stir gently. Refrigerate until ready to serve.

Sparkling Orange Juice

1 gallon orange juice
1 quart champagne, white wine or sparkling juice
Dry ice (if desired)

Make an ice ring with your favorite mold. Place the ring into a punch bowl. Pour in the orange juice and beverage of your choice. You can also pour the liquid ingredients over a small amount of dry ice for a dramatic effect.

Set the punch bowl in the center of a grapevine or evergreen wreath. Place a silk or fresh ivy garland on the wreath and decorate with star garland or berries for a festive look.

Sprinkle the tablecloth with star confetti.

Easy Breakfast Bake

2 1/2 cups cubed or torn bread
1 cup diced lean, cooked ham or
 1 lb. cooked sausage
1 1/2 cups grated cheddar cheese

2 eggs
salt & pepper
2 cups milk

Place bread in a 9" X 11" greased baking dish. Layer ham or sausage and cheese on top of the bread. Combine milk and remaining ingredients, mix and pour over cheese. Cover and refrigerate overnight. Bake, uncovered, at 350° for 30 minutes. Serve warm.

Eggs Extravaganza

4 chopped green onions
2 tbsp. chopped green pepper
1/4 cup chopped mushrooms

6 eggs
butter or margarine
salt & pepper
dry herbs of your choice

Place one tbsp. of butter or margarine in a non stick skillet on medium to medium high heat. Sauté chopped green onions and green pepper. Add mushrooms. Break eggs into the skillet. Add salt and pepper to taste. Stir gently until the eggs are done but not dry. Serve warm.

Decorate a tin or other box to hold all of the photographs from the holidays.

Gather together all of your photos from last year. Put them in albums in January so you can begin saving next year's photos now!!

Shivers Snowman Block of the Month
Applique Drawing

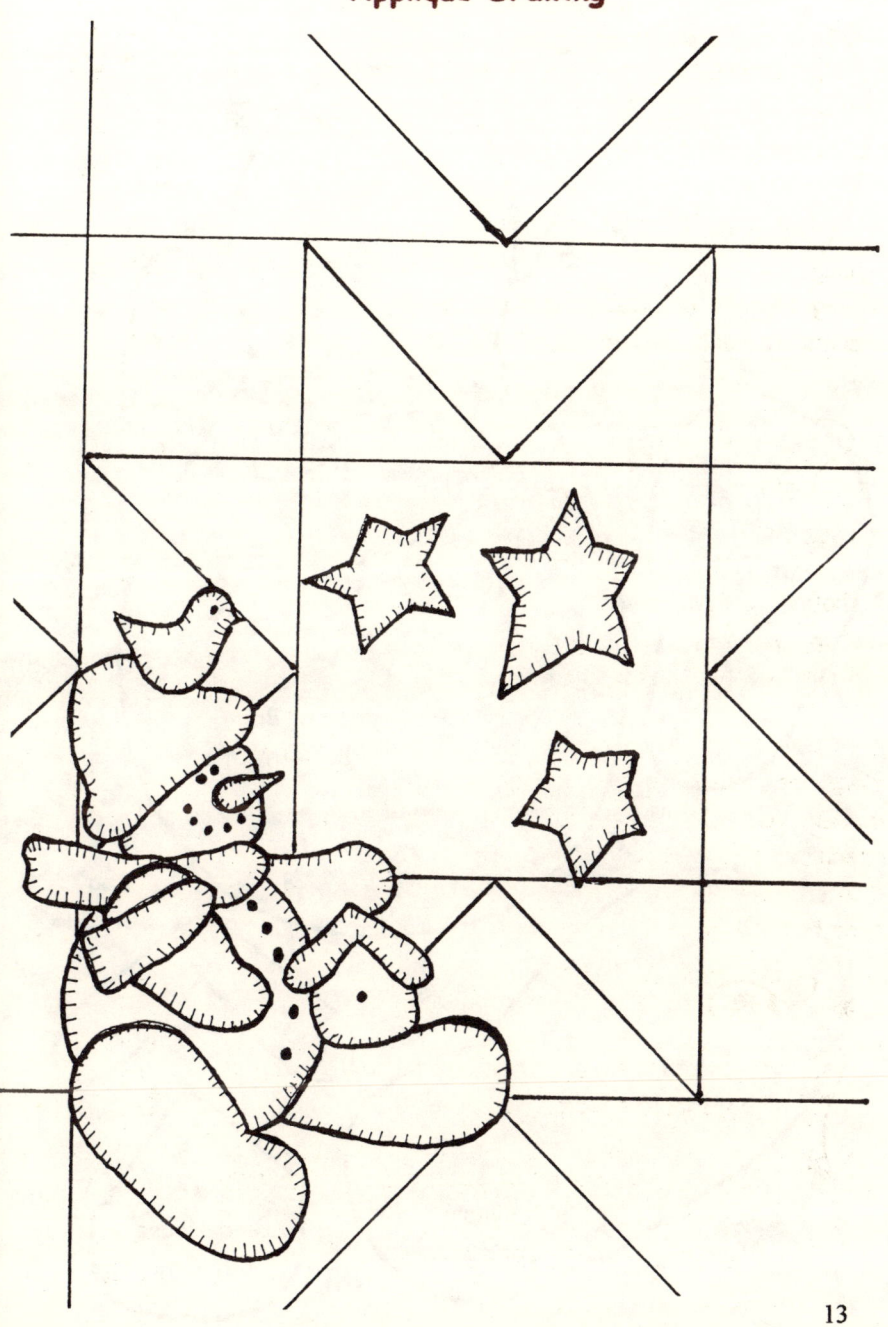

Shivers Snowman Pattern Pieces

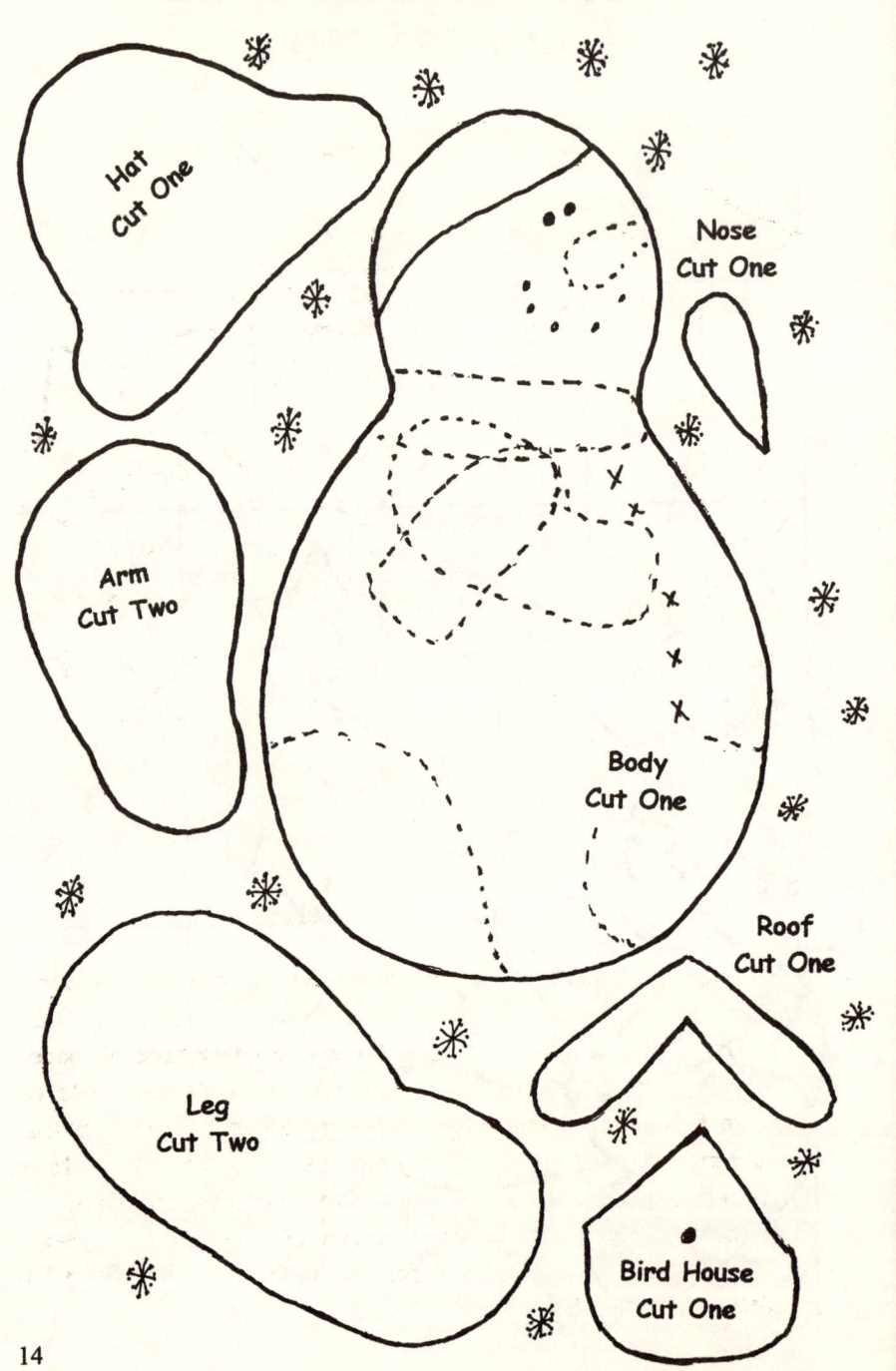

Hat Cut One

Nose Cut One

Arm Cut Two

Body Cut One

Roof Cut One

Leg Cut Two

Bird House Cut One

Shivers Snowman
Remaining Pattern Pieces And Instructions

Star Cut One

Star Cut One

Star Cut One

Bird Cut One

Scarf Cut One (Neck)

Scarf Cut One (Chest)

Instructions:
Make the Double Star Block as instructed on page 16. Trace and cut pattern pieces as stated on each of the patterns. Cut each out of "fused" fabric. (See General Instructions on page 4.) Layer "fused" applique pieces on star block center. (Refer often to full block drawing for placement ideas.) Iron in place. Blanket stitch around each applique piece. Sew French knots on the face for eyes and mouth. Sew additional French knots down the body front for buttons or sew on tiny buttons. Sew a French knot on the bird's head for the eye. (See Stitching Instructions on page 6.)

Double Star Block Construction

Cutting:
Inner Star Block:
From the (Light) Cut One: 5" Center Square
From the (Medium) Cut Four: 2 3/4" X 5" Rectangles
From the (Dark) Cut Eight: 2 3/4" Squares (Star Points)
From the (Medium) Cut Four: 2 3/4" Squares (Corner Squares)
Outer Star:
Center: Inner Star Block (9 1/2" Square)
From the (Medium) Cut Four: 5 " X 9 1/2" Rectangles
From the (Dark) Cut Eight: 5 " Squares (Star Points)
From the (Medium) Cut Four: 5 " Squares (Corner Squares)

Making the Block:
Inner Star Block

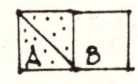

Make Four

#1. Place a 2 3/4" Dark Star Point Square (A) on top of the 2 3/4" X 5" rectangle (B) right sides together. Draw a diagonal line across the square. (A) (See Drawing.) Stitch on the line. Trim seam to 1/4" and press. Repeat this step on the remaining side of the rectangle and on all of the remaining rectangles.
#2. Sew a 2 3/4" corner square (C) to the ends of two rectangles.
#3. Sew the rectangles without the corner squares to the sides of the 5" center block.
#4. Sew the rectangles with the corner squares to the top and bottom. Square to 9 1/2".

Outer Star: (18 1/2" square)
Center: Inner Star Block (Above)
Follow the above instructions using the larger cuts to add the outer star points.

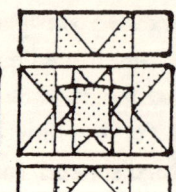

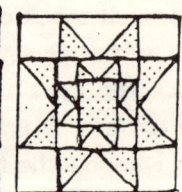

16 For Construction Questions Call 1-800-845-9331

Valentine's Day

Valentine's Day Tea Menu

Chicken Pineapple Almond Salad Sandwiches

Cucumber Sandwiches

Raspberry Salad

Champagne Cranberry Punch

Chocolate Dream Dessert

White Chocolate Chunk Macadamia Cookies

Chocolate Kiss Cookies

Melt My Heart Cookies

**February Hints
And
Angel of My Heart Block of the Month**

Tea Sandwiches

You will need a 3" heart shaped cookie cutter and a variety of sliced breads to cut basic shapes on which the following recipes will be used.

Chicken Pineapple Almond Spread

1 cup cooked finely chopped chicken
1/3 cup well drained crushed pineapple
1/4 cup finely chopped almonds
mayonnaise or salad dressing
 for thinning

Combine all of the ingredients and spread onto heart shaped bread pieces.

Cucumber Sandwiches

thin slices of unpeeled cucumber
softened butter or margarine
mayonnaise or salad dressing
fresh parsley

Spread heart shaped breads with softened butter or margarine, mayonnaise and/or salad dressing. Place the cucumber slices on a bread piece and place a small sprig of parsley on each.

Make a center piece for your Valentine tea by placing a collection of "Old" but loved tea cups on a mirror. Fill the cups with small plants, potpourri or even small votive candles. Twine fresh or silk greens and ribbon among the cups to finish.

Red Raspberry Salad

1 package raspberry gelatin (3 oz.)
1 cup boiling water
1 package frozen raspberries, undrained (10 oz.)
2 1/2 cups sour cream
1/2 cup mayonnaise
2 tbsp. sugar
1 package cherry gelatin (3 oz.)
1 cup boiling water
1 can crushed pineapple, drained (20 oz.)
1 can whole cranberry sauce (16 oz.)

Dissolve raspberry gelatin in 1 cup of hot water. Add raspberries to gelatin until the raspberries are separated. Pour into a 9" X 13" pan. Refrigerate to set. Spread sour cream over surface of set gelatin. Dissolve cherry gelatin in remaining 1 cup of hot water. Stir in crushed pineapple and cranberry sauce. Stir well. Cool to room temperature. Spoon mixture over sour cream layer. Cover and refrigerate until serving time. Cut into squares to serve. Stir mayonnaise, sugar and remaining sour cream together. Put a tablespoon of this mixture on each square when served.

Cleaning your home while your children are
growing is like shoveling snow while it is snowing!

Champagne Cranberry Punch

Ice Ring:
3 to 4 cup mold. Fresh strawberries or maraschino cherries. Place fruit in the bottom of the mold. Add enough water to just cover the fruit. Freeze until the water covering fruit is set. Add enough water to fill the mold. To remove, run warm water over the outer sides of mold and place in a festive bowl.

Punch:
4 cups chilled cranberry juice
1 bottle champagne or sparkling grape juice
Combine juices and pour over the ice ring.

Chocolate Dream Dessert

Crust:
1 cup flour
1/2 cup chopped nuts
1/2 cup melted butter

First Layer:
1 package cream cheese (8 oz.)
1 cup powdered sugar
1 cup Cool Whip
 (remaining used for topping)

Second Layer:
2 packages instant chocolate pudding (3 oz.)
3 cups milk
1/2 tsp. vanilla

Blend flour, nuts and butter. Pat in a 9" X 13" pan. Bake 15 minutes at 325°. Cool Crust. First Layer: Stir cream cheese, powdered sugar and Cool Whip together. Spread on cooled crust. Second Layer: Stir second layer ingredients together and carefully spread mixture over first layer. Spread remaining Cool Whip on top. Sprinkle with chopped nuts to finish. Refrigerate. Serve cold.

White Chocolate Chunk Macadamia Cookies

1 cup butter
1 cup light brown sugar
1/2 cup sugar
2 eggs
1 tsp. vanilla
2 1/4 cups flour

1 tsp. baking powder
1 tsp. salt
1 cup macadamia nuts (coarsely chopped)
2 cups chocolate or almond bark (broken into bite size pieces)

Cream butter and sugars until light and fluffy. Beat in eggs and vanilla. Combine flour, baking soda, and salt. Gradually stir dry ingredients into creamed mixture. Stir in nuts and chocolate pieces. Drop by heaping teaspoonfuls onto greased baking sheets. Bake in a preheated oven at 350°, 10 to 12 minutes. Cool slightly before removing from sheets. Makes about 6 dozen cookies.

Melt My Heart Cookies

Cookies:
1 cup butter or margarine (softened)
1/3 cup powdered sugar
1 tsp. vanilla
2/3 cup cornstarch
1 cup flour

Icing:
1 1/2 cup powdered sugar
2 tsp. softened butter
orange juice

Mix cookie ingredients together and drop by teaspoonfuls onto an ungreased cookie sheet. Bake at 350°, 8 to 10 minutes, until very light tan. Cool and frost with icing.

Icing:
Mix butter and powdered sugar together. Stir in enough juice to make icing thin. Drizzle the icing over each cookie.

Angel of My Heart Block of the Month
Applique Drawing

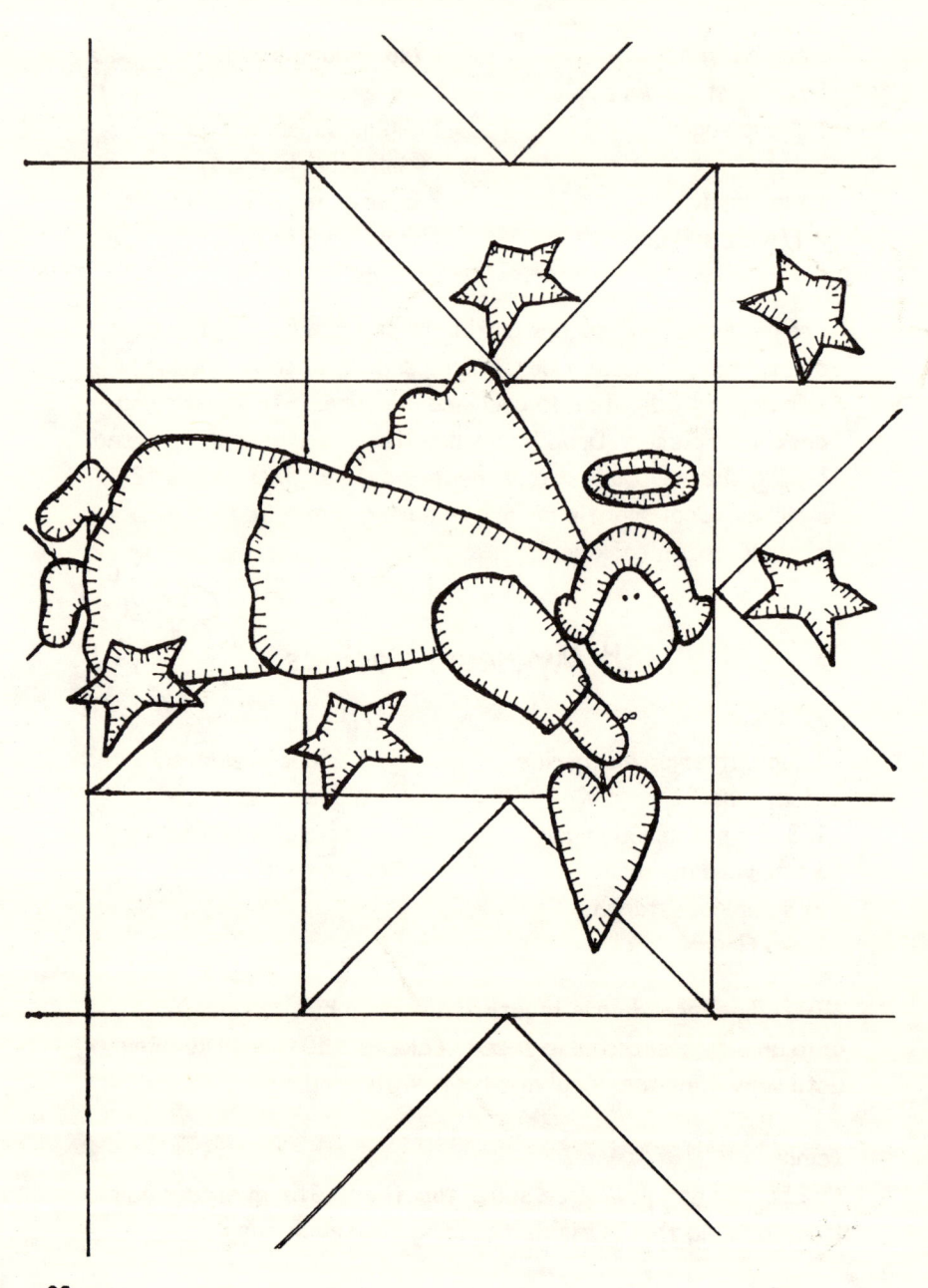

Angel of My Heart Pattern Pieces

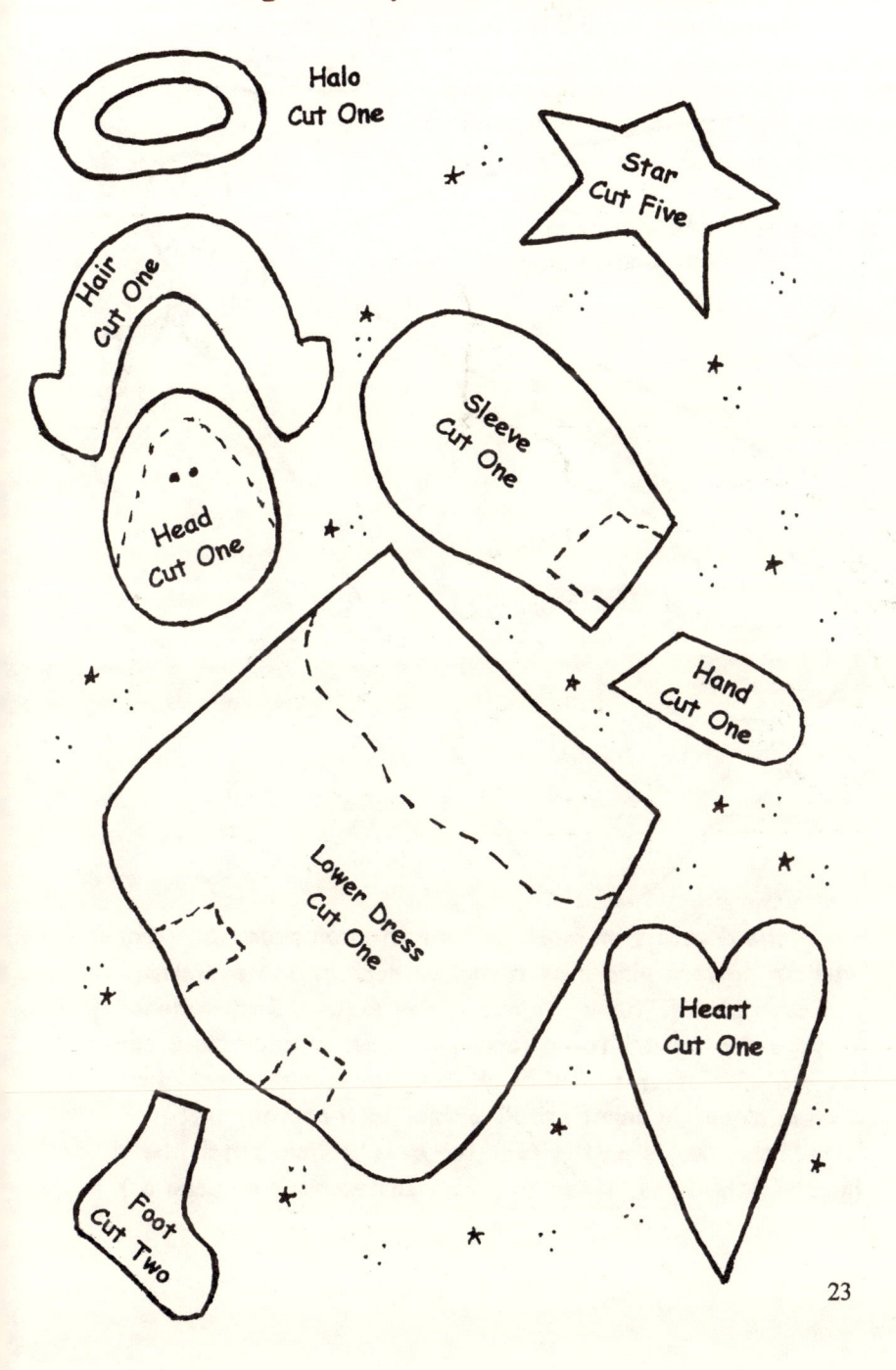

Halo
Cut One

Star
Cut Five

Hair
Cut One

Sleeve
Cut One

Head
Cut One

Hand
Cut One

Lower Dress
Cut One

Heart
Cut One

Foot
Cut Two

Angel of My Heart
Remaining Pattern Pieces and Instructions

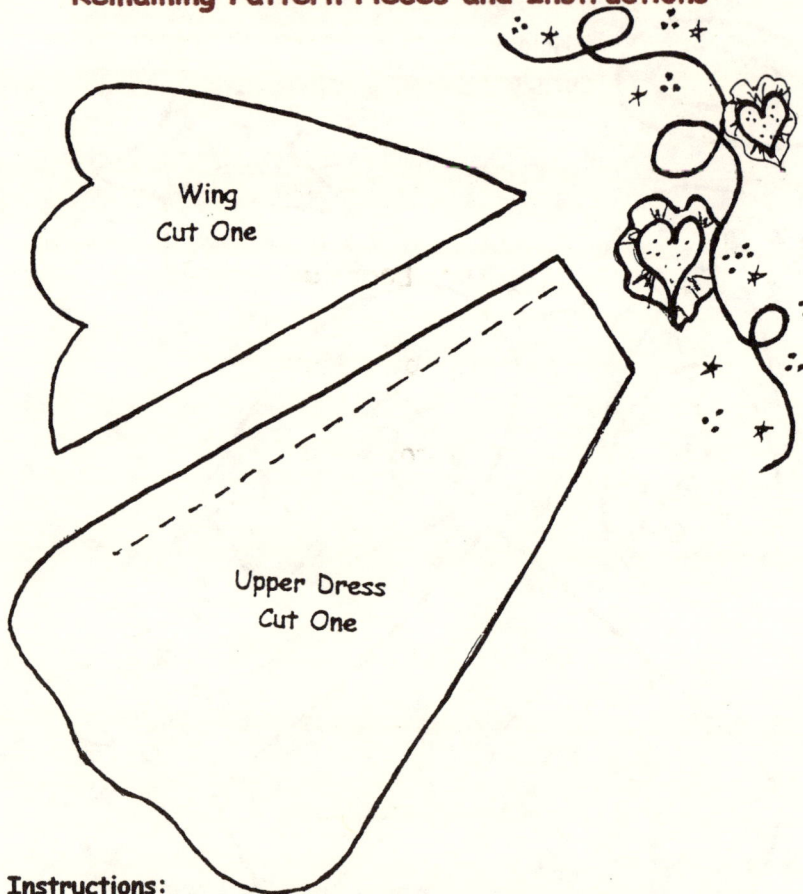

Wing
Cut One

Upper Dress
Cut One

Instructions:
Make the double star block as instructed on page 16. Trace and cut pattern pieces as stated on each of the patterns. Cut each out of "fused" fabric. (See General Instructions on page 4.) Layer "fused" applique pieces on star block center. (Refer often to full block drawing for placement ideas.) Iron in place. Blanket stitch around each applique piece. Sew French knots on the face for eyes. Chain stitch the heart to the hand. (See Stitching Instructions on page 6.)

St. Patrick's Day

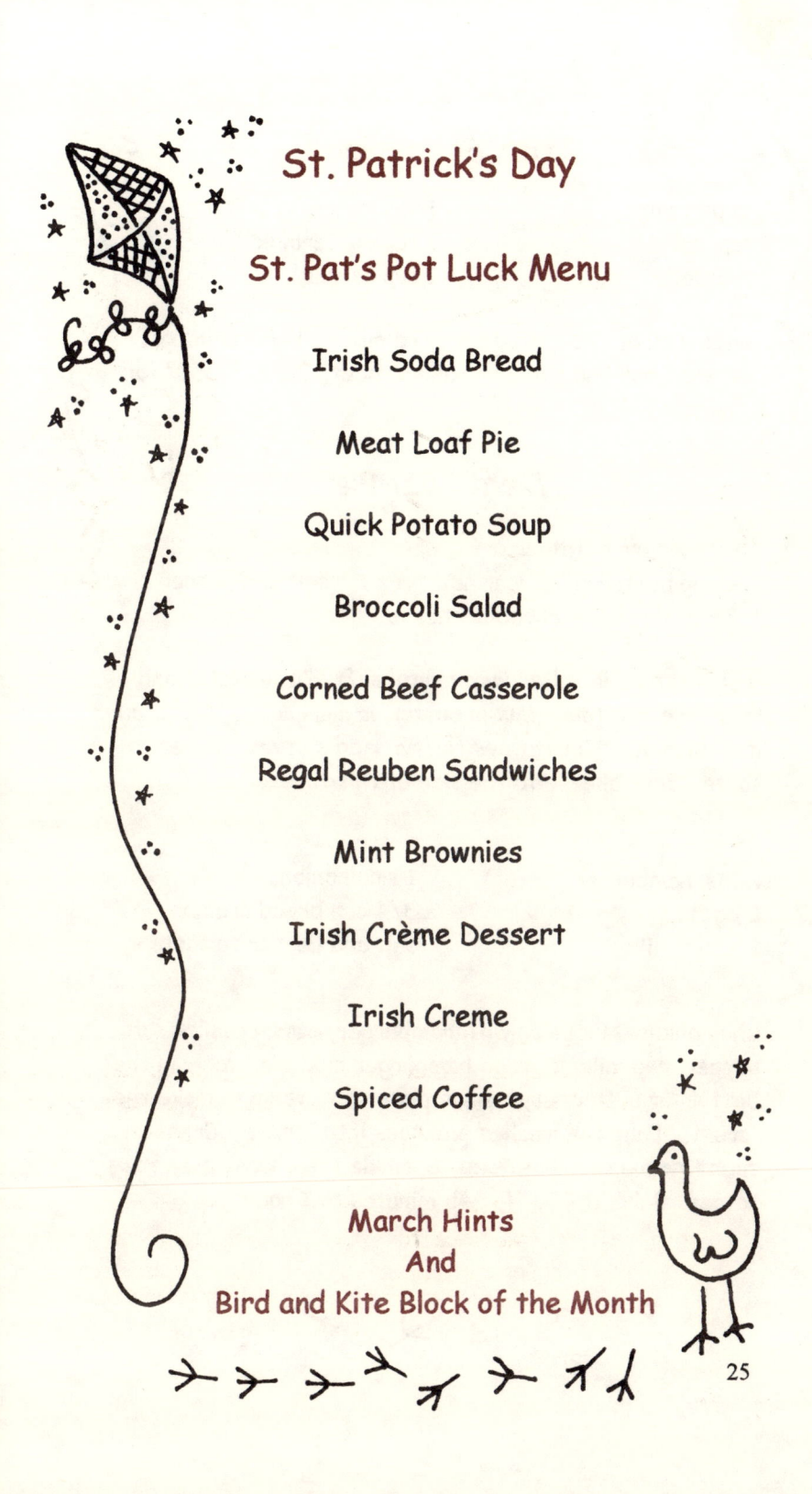

St. Pat's Pot Luck Menu

Irish Soda Bread

Meat Loaf Pie

Quick Potato Soup

Broccoli Salad

Corned Beef Casserole

Regal Reuben Sandwiches

Mint Brownies

Irish Crème Dessert

Irish Creme

Spiced Coffee

March Hints
And
Bird and Kite Block of the Month

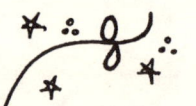

Irish Soda Bread

2 cups flour
1 tsp. salt
1 tsp. soda
1/2 tsp. baking powder
1 cup buttermilk
1 cup raisins

Combine all of the ingredients and mix well. Form into a flattened ball and place on baking sheet. Bake at 350° for 30 minutes.

Meat Loaf Pie

4 - 5 medium potatoes
1/4 cup butter or margarine
1/2 cup shredded cheddar cheese
milk
salt and pepper

Boil potatoes in salted water until soft. Drain water and mash the potatoes. Mix in butter or margarine. Add enough milk to make the potatoes fluffy. Add salt and pepper to taste. Save cheese to the side at this time.

Crust:
2 lbs. hamburger
2 eggs
1/2 cup milk
1 small onion
3/4 cup bread crumbs
salt and pepper to taste

Chop onion. Mix onion with hamburger, eggs, crumbs, salt, pepper and milk. Spread hamburger mixture evenly in the bottom of a 9" deep dish pie plate. Pat evenly to make the "crust". Pour the mashed potatoes into "crust". Create a slight mound with potatoes. Sprinkle the cheese over the potatoes. Bake at 400° for 45 minutes to 1 hour.

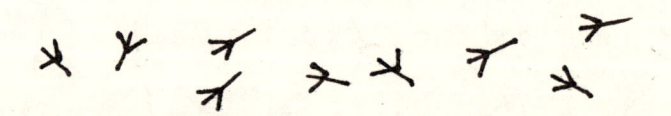

Quick Potato Soup

2 -3 grated potatoes
2 tbsp. grated onion
1 can evaporated milk (11 oz.)
2 cups milk

4 tbsp. water
2 tbsp. flour
2 tbsp. parsley
salt and pepper to taste

Cover potatoes and onions with water and boil until done. Do not drain. Add evaporated milk and milk. Cook over medium heat, stirring constantly, until hot. Thicken by stirring the flour and water together until you have a smooth paste. Stir the paste into the soup until it is the thickness you desire. Add salt and pepper to taste. Stir in parsley.

Broccoli Salad

1 medium head broccoli
4 slices crisp-fried bacon, crumbled
1/4 cup chopped green onions
1/4 cup raisins

1/4 cup sunflower seeds
1/2 cup mayonnaise
1 tbsp. vinegar
1/4 cup sugar

Wash and clean the vegetables. Cut broccoli tops only into small pieces. Combine all remaining ingredients in a bowl. Mix thoroughly. Chill and serve.

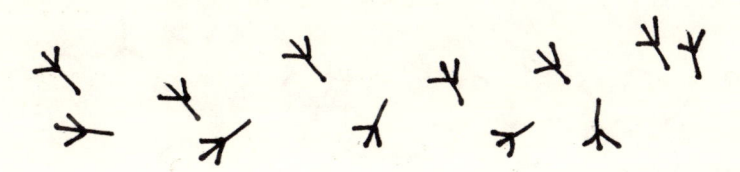

Corned Beef Casserole

1 can corned beef
1 can cream of mushroom soup
milk
1/2 lb. American cheese (cubed)
1/2 cup chopped onion
1 package noodles (8 oz.)
1/2 cup bread crumbs

Mix soup, milk, onions and cheese in a saucepan. Cook over medium heat until the cheese is melted. Cook the noodles as stated on the package. Drain and stir in the corned beef. Place the noodles and corned beef in a casserole dish. Pour the cheese mixture over the noodles. Top with crumbs. Bake one hour at 300°.

Regal Reuben Sandwich

thin sliced corned beef
sliced Swiss cheese
butter
sauerkraut
sliced rye bread

Butter the outer sides of two bread slices. Layer the thinly sliced corned beef, sauerkraut and cheese between the bread slices. Fry in a heated skillet until the cheese melts and the bread is toasted on both sides.

Notes:

Mint Brownies

1 can Hershey syrup (16 oz.)
1 cup sugar
1 tsp. vanilla
1/2 cup butter
4 eggs
1 cup flour
1/2 tsp. salt

Topping:
1/2 cup butter, melted
2 cups powdered sugar
2 tbsp. Crème de menthe
1 cup chocolate chips
  (melted)
milk

Mix the sugar, syrup, vanilla, melted butter and eggs together until smooth. Stir in flour and salt. Bake in a 9" X 13" pan at 350° for 30 minutes. Cool. To make topping, mix butter, powdered sugar, Crème de menthe and melted chocolate chips together. Add enough milk to make topping thin enough to spread. Spread topping evenly over brownies.

Irish Crème Dessert

3 tbsp. cold water
1 envelope unflavored gelatin
2 cups whipping cream
1/2 cup Irish Creme liqueur

1/2 cup sugar
1/2 cup finely chopped semisweet or
  bittersweet chocolate,
  reserve 2 tbsp. for garnish

In a small heat proof bowl, combine water and gelatin. Allow to sit 5 minutes to soften gelatin. Place the bowl in a saucepan of water over low heat and stir until the gelatin is dissolved. Remove from heat and cool to room temperature.
In a large mixing bowl, whip cream until soft peaks form. Blend in liqueur and sugar. Fold in chocolate. Spoon into individual glasses and chill at least 1 hour. Sprinkle with remaining chocolate on top of each dessert when served.

Spiced Coffee Mix

4 cups firmly packed brown sugar
2 cups coffee flavored liqueur
1 1/2 cups non-dairy powdered creamer
1 1/2 tsp. cinnamon
1 tsp. ground allspice

In a large bowl combine and mix all of the above ingredients together. Cover and chill. To serve, spoon one tbsp. coffee into a mug. Add 6 ounces of hot coffee, cocoa or milk. Store coffee mix in an airtight container in the refrigerator.

Irish Crème

1 3/4 cup brandy, rum or Irish whiskey
1 can sweetened condensed milk (14 oz.)
1 cup whipping cream
4 eggs
2 tbsp. chocolate syrup
2 tbsp. instant coffee
1 tsp. vanilla

Blend all ingredients together, refrigerate. Shake before serving. Makes 5 cups. Makes a great gift!!!

The Bird and Kite Block of the Month
Applique Drawing

The Bird and Kite Pattern Pieces

Bird Cut One

Beak Cut One

Heart Cut One

The Bird and Kite
Remaining Pattern Pieces

Kite Cut One

Kite Cut One

Kite Cut One

Kite Cut One

Star Cut One

33

The Bird and Kite
Block of the Month Instructions

Instructions:

Make the double star block as instructed on page 16. Trace And cut pattern pieces as stated on each of the patterns. Cut each out of "fused" fabric. (See General Instructions on page 4.) Layer "fused" applique pieces on star block center. (Refer often to full block drawing for placement ideas.)

Iron in place. Blanket stitch around each applique piece. Sew French knots on the face for eyes. Chain stitch the heart to the hand. (See Stitching Instructions on page 6.)

Throw Pillows:

To make any of the double star blocks into throw pillows simply follow all of the instructions given for each block. Cut a piece of fabric 18" square. Place block and 18" fabric right sides together. Sew around leaving an opening for stuffing or inserting a pre-made pillow form. Turn the pillow cover right side out. Press. Insert stuffing or pillow form. Hand sew the opening shut. These make great home-dec items as well as gifts or bazaar items.

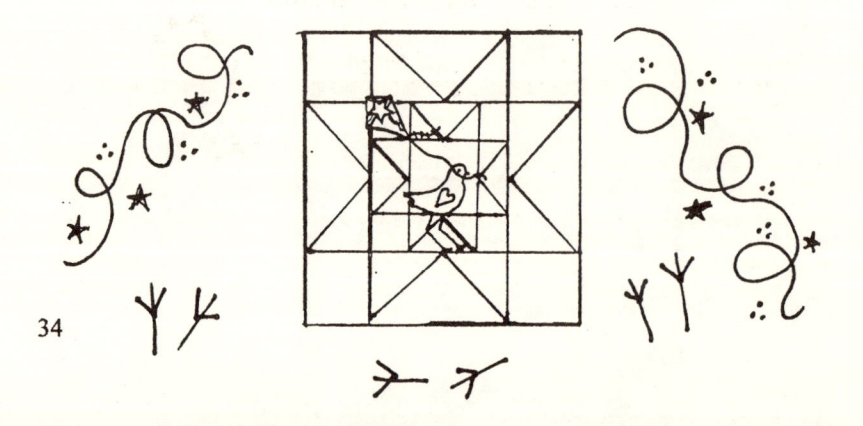

Easter

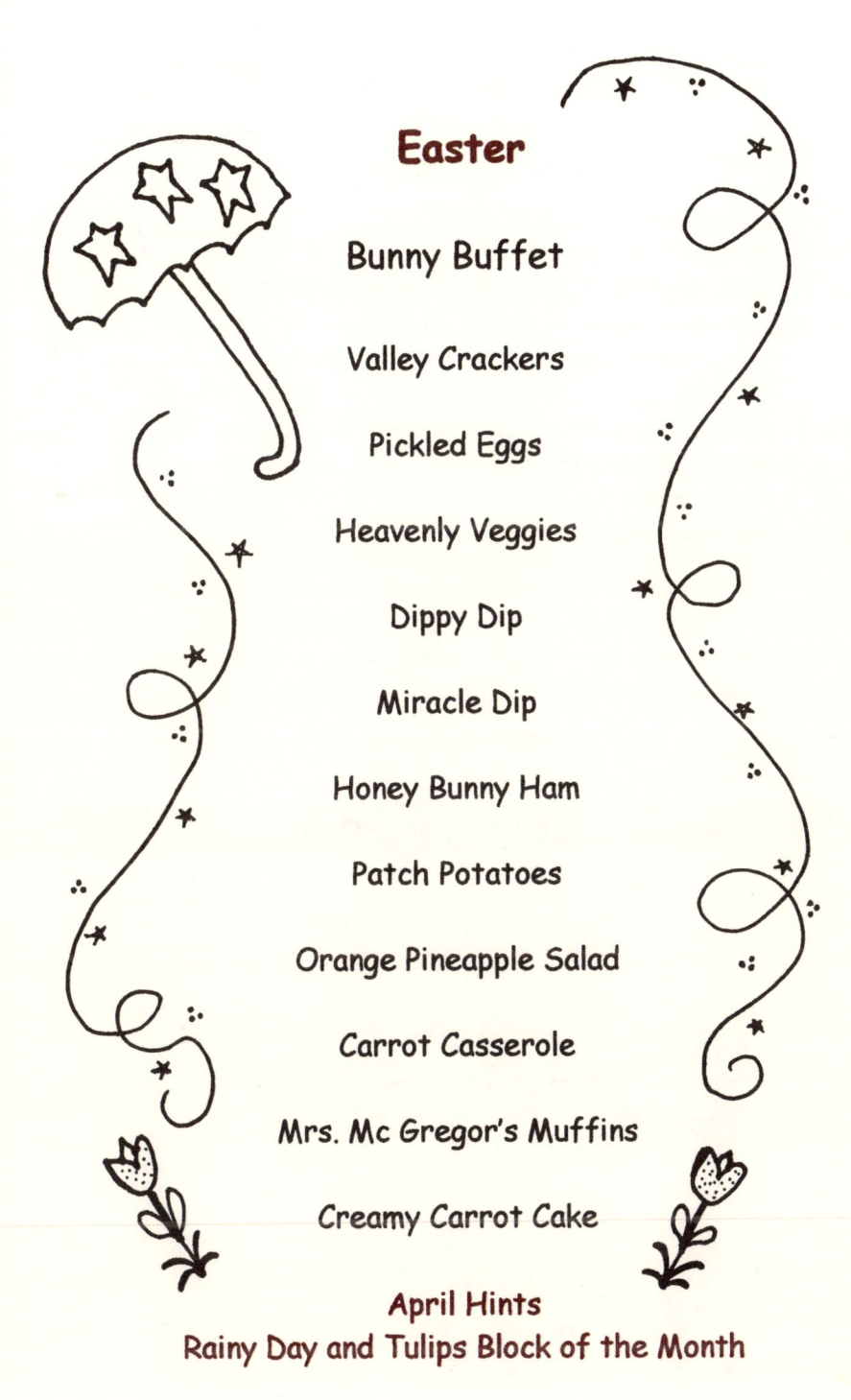

Bunny Buffet

Valley Crackers

Pickled Eggs

Heavenly Veggies

Dippy Dip

Miracle Dip

Honey Bunny Ham

Patch Potatoes

Orange Pineapple Salad

Carrot Casserole

Mrs. Mc Gregor's Muffins

Creamy Carrot Cake

April Hints
Rainy Day and Tulips Block of the Month

Valley Crackers

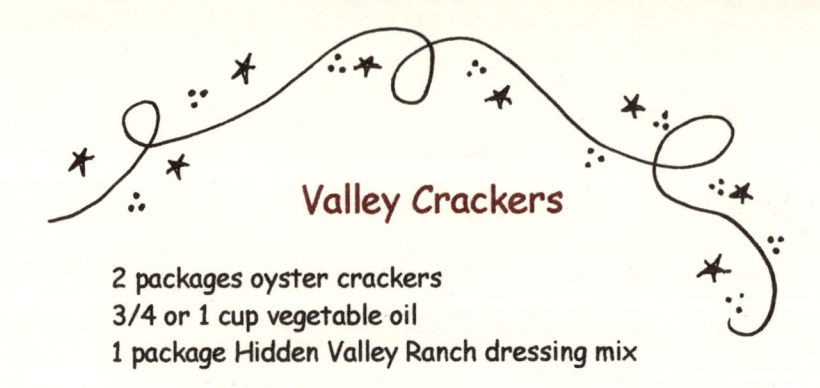

2 packages oyster crackers
3/4 or 1 cup vegetable oil
1 package Hidden Valley Ranch dressing mix

Put the crackers in a large bowl. Sprinkle on the dressing, Stir in the oil. Let set a few hours before serving. Serve as an appetizer or with soups and vegetables.

Pickled Eggs

3 dozen eggs, boiled and peeled
1 jar hot chili peppers, chopped
1 cup water
1 tsp. salt
4 bay leaves

Place eggs in a clean gallon jar. Mix the remaining ingredients together and pour over eggs. Refrigerate for a few days before serving.

Heavenly Veggies

carrots
celery
cucumbers
party type toothpicks

green onions
cauliflower
broccoli
1 loaf of Hawaiian bread

Clean and cut vegetables into serving sizes. Push the party type toothpicks through each vegetable piece. Hollow out the center of Hawaiian bread to make a bowl. Place the bread "bowl" onto a platter. Push the pick ends into the outer crust of the bread. Fill the "bowl" with any of the following dips.

Dippy Dip

1 cup sour cream
2 cups real mayonnaise
1 tbsp. parsley flakes

2 tsp. seasoning salt
1 tbsp. dill weed
3 tbsp. onion flakes

Mix the above ingredients together until creamy. Chill and serve.

Miracle Dip

1/2 cup sour cream
1/2 cup Miracle Whip
1/2 cup chili sauce
2 tsp. yellow mustard
1 tbsp. horseradish

1 tbsp. chives
1 tsp. Worcestershire sauce
2 drops Tabasco sauce
1 tsp. sugar

Mix all of the ingredients in a medium sized bowl. Stir until creamy. Chill before serving.

Honey Bunny Ham

1 five -six pound cooked ham
1 cup orange juice
1 can whole cranberry sauce (16 oz.)
1 can jellied cranberry sauce (16 oz.)
1/2 cup honey

1 can mandarin oranges slices drained (11 oz.)
2 tsp. seasoned salt
2 1/2 tsp. seasoned pepper
1 tsp. garlic powder

Preheat oven to 350°. Place ham in a shallow baking dish. Bake 1 hour. Remove from oven and pour off juices. Combine the remaining ingredients in a large sauce pan. Bring to a boil. Reduce heat to low. Cook for 30 minutes stirring occasionally. Spoon the sauce over ham coating it well. Bake 30 minutes longer. Serve with remaining sauce.

Patch Potatoes

5 cups diced peeled potatoes
4 green onions
1 cup creamed cottage cheese
3/4 - 1 cup shredded Cheddar cheese

1 cup sour cream
1/2 tsp. salt
pepper to taste

Place potatoes and onions in a covered 2 1/2 quart microwavable casserole. Microwave on high for 10 to 11 minutes or until the potatoes are tender. Let stand covered. Combine next four ingredients in a medium sized bowl. Stir in potatoes. Sprinkle cheese over the top of the potato mixture in a patchwork pattern. Cover loosely with plastic wrap and microwave on high 1 to 2 minutes or until the cheese is melted. Let stand 2 minutes before serving.

Orange Pineapple Salad

1 can crushed pineapple and juice (20 oz.)
1 pkg. orange gelatin (3 oz.)
1 cup heavy cream
1/4 cup sugar
1 cup cottage cheese

Drain pineapple, reserving juice in a small saucepan. Add enough water to make 1 1/3 cups liquid. Bring to a boil. Place gelatin in a bowl. Add boiling liquid and stir until gelatin is dissolved. Let cool until slightly thickened. Whip cream until peaks form. Slowly fold in the sugar. Stir in pineapple and cottage cheese and gelatin. Blend well. Pour into a 1 1/2 qt. serving bowl. Chill 3 hours to overnight before serving.

Carrot Casserole

1 onion chopped
3 tbsp. butter or margarine
4 cups sliced cooked carrots
1 can cream of celery soup
salt and pepper to taste
1/2 cup shredded Cheddar cheese
3 cups herb flavored stuffing
1/3 cup melted butter

Preheat oven to 350°. Sauté onion in 3 tsp. butter in a large skillet. Stir in carrots, soup, salt, pepper and cheese. Spoon into 2-quart baking dish. Top with stuffing mix and 1/3 cup melted butter mixed together. Bake 20 minutes.

Mrs. Mc Gregor's Muffins

2 cubes butter
4 large eggs
4 tsp. baking powder
4 cups flour
1 1/2 cups sugar
2 tsp. vanilla
1/2 tsp. salt
1 cup milk
1/2 cup each of three different berries

Mix above ingredients except the berries. Do not over mix. Divide dough into thirds and gently fold in berries of your choice. Bake in paper lined muffin pan at 375° for 25 minutes.

Creamy Carrot Cake

2 cups sugar
2 cups flour
2 tsp. baking soda
2 tsp. cinnamon
salt to taste
1 1/4 cups vegetable oil

4 eggs, slightly beaten
3 1/2 cups lightly packed
   finely shredded carrots
2 tsp. vanilla
Cream Cheese Icing

Preheat oven to 350°. Mix sugar, flour, baking soda, cinnamon and salt in a large bowl. Blend in oil. Add vanilla, eggs and carrots. Blend just until evenly mixed. Pour into a 10" spring form pan greased and lightly floured. Bake for 45 minutes to one hour. Let cool. Frost with Cream Cheese Icing.

Cream Cheese Icing

1 package cream cheese (8 oz.)
1/2 cup butter or margarine
16 ounces powdered sugar

1 tsp. vanilla
1 tsp. orange juice
1 tbsp. grated orange
   rind

Blend softened cream cheese and butter in a small bowl. Add sugar slowly, beating until smooth and creamy. Add remaining ingredients, blending well. Thin with additional orange juice if necessary. Spread on cooled cake.

Rainy Day and Tulips Block of the Month
Applique Drawing

Rainy Day and Tulips Pattern Pieces

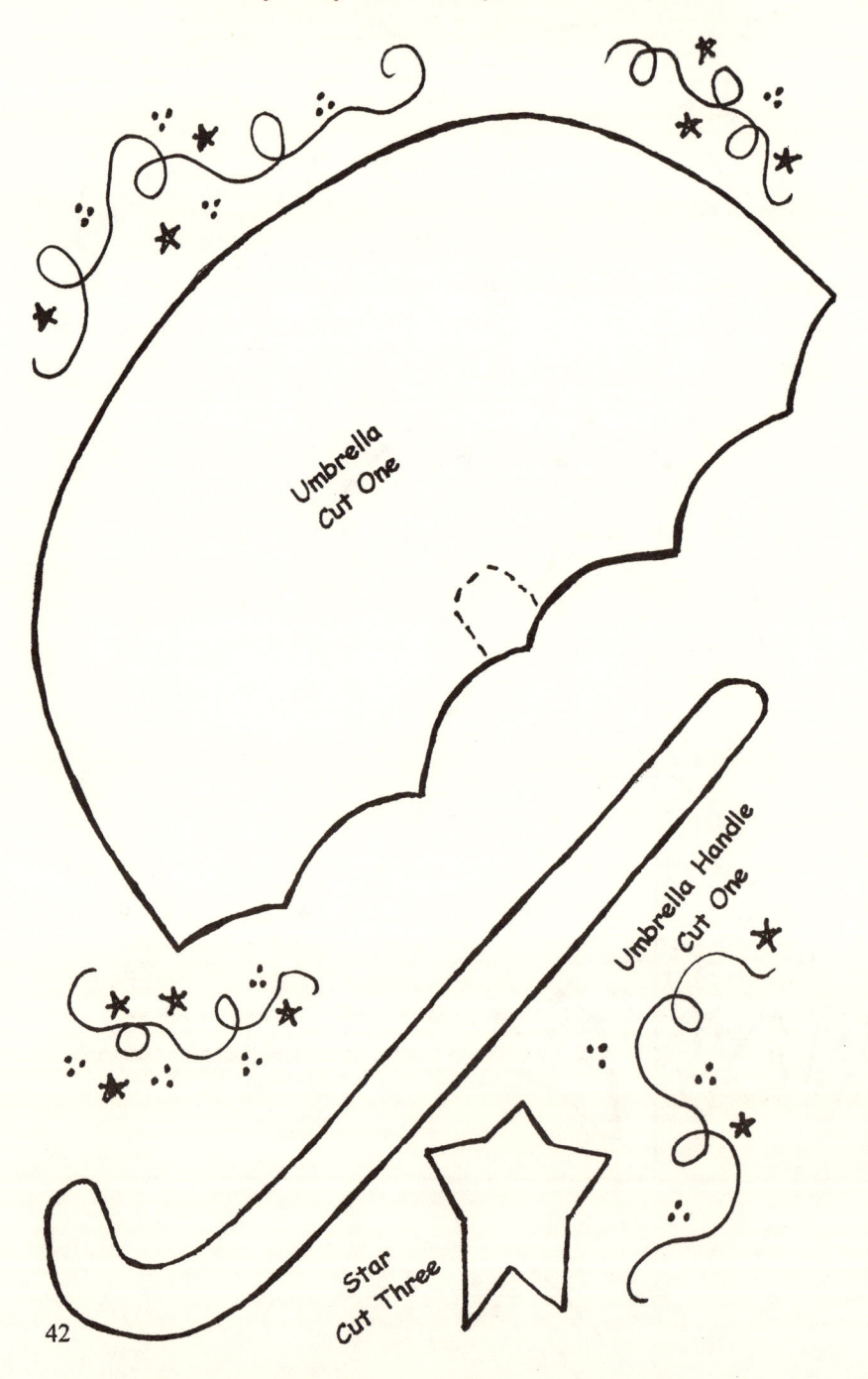

Umbrella
Cut One

Umbrella Handle
Cut One

Star
Cut Three

42

Rainy Day and Tulips
Remaining Pattern Pieces and Instructions

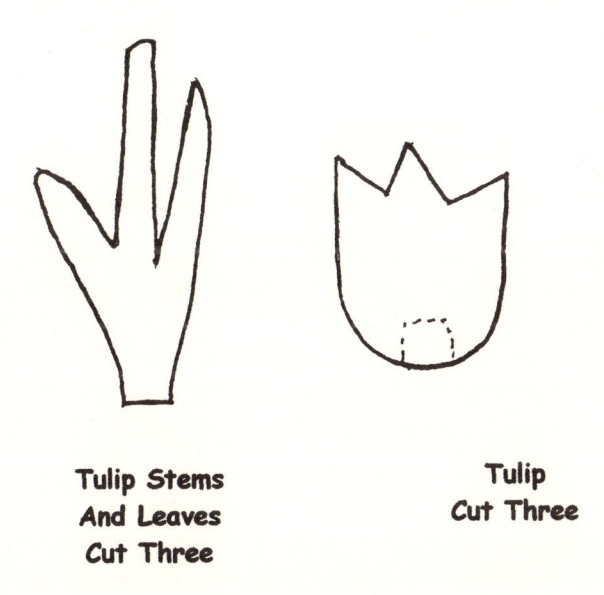

Tulip Stems
And Leaves
Cut Three

Tulip
Cut Three

Make the Double Star Block as instructed on page 16. Trace and cut pattern pieces as stated on each of the patterns. Cut each out of "fused" fabric. (See General Instructions on page 4.) Layer "fused" applique pieces on the star block center. (Refer often to full block drawing for placement ideas.) Iron in place. Blanket stitch around each applique piece. (See Stitching Instructions on page 6.)

Notes:

Mother's Day

Love You Lunch Menu

Hot Chicken Salad

Lemon Tea Muffins

Glazed Fruit Pizza

Little Italy Salad

Satin Slipper Pie

Cheese Cake Bits

Strawberry Pie

Vanilla Wafers

May Hints
And
Mother's Day Basket Block of the Month

Hot Chicken Salad

4 cups cut up cooked chicken
2 red pimentos, finely chopped
1 tbsp. onion, finely chopped
3/4 cup mayonnaise
1 tsp. salt
4 hard boiled eggs, diced
2 cups celery, chopped
3/4 cup cream of chicken soup

Topping:
1 cup shredded mild Cheddar cheese
1 1/2 cups crushed potato chips
2/3 cup chopped toasted almonds

Combine the chicken, pimentos, onion, mayonnaise, salt, eggs, celery and soup in a 9" X 13" casserole dish. Stir cheese, potato chips and almonds together in a small bowl. Sprinkle the cheese mixture over top of the casserole evenly. Refrigerate covered overnight. Bake at 350° for 25 to 30 minutes or until bubbly.

Lemon Tea Muffins

1 cup flour
1 tsp. baking powder
1/4 tsp. salt
1/2 cup margarine
1/2 cup sugar
2 eggs, separated
3 tbsp. lemon juice
1 tsp. grated lemon peel
2 tbsp. sugar
1/4 tsp. vanilla

Preheat oven to 375°. Stir flour, baking powder and salt together in a large bowl. Cream margarine and sugar together in another bowl until light and fluffy. Beat egg yolks and blend into the creamed ingredients. Add dry ingredients alternately with lemon juice. Do not over mix. Beat egg whites stiff. Fold the egg whites and lemon peel into batter gently. Fill muffin papers or greased muffin tins 2/3 full. Bake 20 - 25 minutes. (Top with a combination of cinnamon and sugar if desired.)

Divine Chicken Divan

2 packages frozen broccoli spears, slightly thawed (10 oz.)
6 cooked boneless skinless chicken breasts
salt and pepper to taste
1/2 cup butter or margarine
1 package cream cheese (8 oz.)
1/2 cup mayonnaise

Preheat oven to 350°. Place broccoli in a 9" X 13" casserole. Arrange chicken on broccoli. Sprinkle with salt and pepper. Melt butter or margarine in a medium skillet over medium heat. Stir in remaining ingredients. Heat, stirring frequently until cheese is melted and the mixture is smooth and creamy. Pour over chicken. Bake 35 minutes until bubbly and broccoli is tender crisp.

Luscious Lemon Chicken

1/2 cup margarine
juice of one lemon
1 tsp. poultry seasoning

4 skinless boneless
chicken breast halves
fresh parsley

Melt margarine in a small saucepan. Add lemon juice and poultry seasoning. Mix well. Place chicken breasts in a greased ovenproof dish. Pour margarine mixture over top and bake at 350° for one hour. Serve with lemon slices and fresh parsley.

Glazed Fruit Pizza

1 package sugar cookie dough (20 oz.)
1 package cream cheese (8 oz.)
1 cup sugar
1 tsp. vanilla
fresh or canned fruit, sliced

1 1/2 tbsp. cornstarch
6 tbsp. water
1/2 cup orange juice
2 tbsp. lemon juice

Preheat oven to 350°. Coat 9" X 13" baking dish with nonstick cooking spray or vegetable oil. Slice cookie dough. Press dough into prepared dish to make crust. Bake 10 to 15 minutes or until lightly browned. Let cool completely. Combine softened cream cheese, 1/2 cup sugar and vanilla. Spread on crust. Top with sliced fruit. Bring juices to a boil. Mix cornstarch and water together. Add the cornstarch mixture to the juices. Cook until thick. Let cool. Spread over pizza and serve.

Little Italy Salad

2 large beefsteak tomatoes, sliced
6-8 oz. mozzarella cheese, sliced
1 small red onion, sliced
salt and pepper to taste

1/4 cup extra-virgin olive oil
1 Tbsp. chopped green Greek
   olives
1 Tbsp. fresh basil leaves
sunflower seeds if desired

Arrange tomato slices and mozzarella cheese alternately in a circle on the serving plate. Place onion ring slices in the middle of the circle. Sprinkle salt and pepper over the salad. Drizzle with olive oil. Sprinkle with olives, Basil and sunflower seeds.

Mothers Are God's Special Angels

Satin Slipper Pie

20 marshmallows
1/2 cup milk
6 milk chocolate candy bars
1 cup heavy whipping cream
1 baked 9-inch pie shell
toasted almonds

Combine the first 3 ingredients in a medium saucepan. Heat over medium to medium high heat until melted. Let cool. Whip cream and fold into cooled mixture. Pour into pie shell. Chill until firm. Garnish with toasted almonds.

Cheese Cake Bits

1 cup flour
1/2 cup chopped pecans
1/3 cup firmly packed light brown sugar
1/3 cup butter or margarine, melted
1 package cream cheese, softened (8 oz.)
1/4 cup sugar
1 egg
2 tbsp. milk
1 tbsp. lemon juice
1 tsp. vanilla extract

Combine flour, pecans, and brown sugar in a medium bowl. Stir in melted butter until blended. Reserve 1/3 cup of mixture. Press remainder in the bottom of an 8-inch square baking pan. Bake in a 350° oven for 12-15 minutes. Beat cream cheese and sugar until smooth. Beat in remaining ingredients. Pour over baked crust. Sprinkle with reserved pecan mixture. Return to oven and bake 25 minutes. Cool slightly. Cut into 2-inch squares.

Strawberry Surprise

1 pint strawberries
1 large banana
grated orange peel of one orange
1 1/2 cups whipping cream
1 tbsp. powdered sugar

Place strawberries in a large bowl. Place banana and orange peel in a blender. Blend until smooth. Whip whipping cream in a chilled bowl until soft peaks form. Add powdered sugar gradually. Fold in strawberries and blended mixture. Pour into frosted dessert glasses. Chill until ready to serve.

Vanilla Wafers

1 cup butter
1/3 cup whipping cream
2 cups flour
sugar

Topping:
1/4 cup butter, softened
3/4 cup powdered sugar
1 egg yolk
1 tsp. vanilla
1/4 tsp. almond extract

Heat oven to 375°. Mix butter, cream and flour. Chill one hour. Roll dough on a lightly floured board to a 1/8" thickness. Cut into 1 1/2" rounds. Dip both sides in sugar and bake on an ungreased cookie sheet 7 to 9 minutes or until slightly puffy. Let cool. Mix remaining ingredients together until smooth and creamy. Spread topping on one half of the cookies. Top with the remaining cookies.

Mother's Day Basket Block of the Month
Applique Drawing

Mother's Day Basket Pattern Pieces

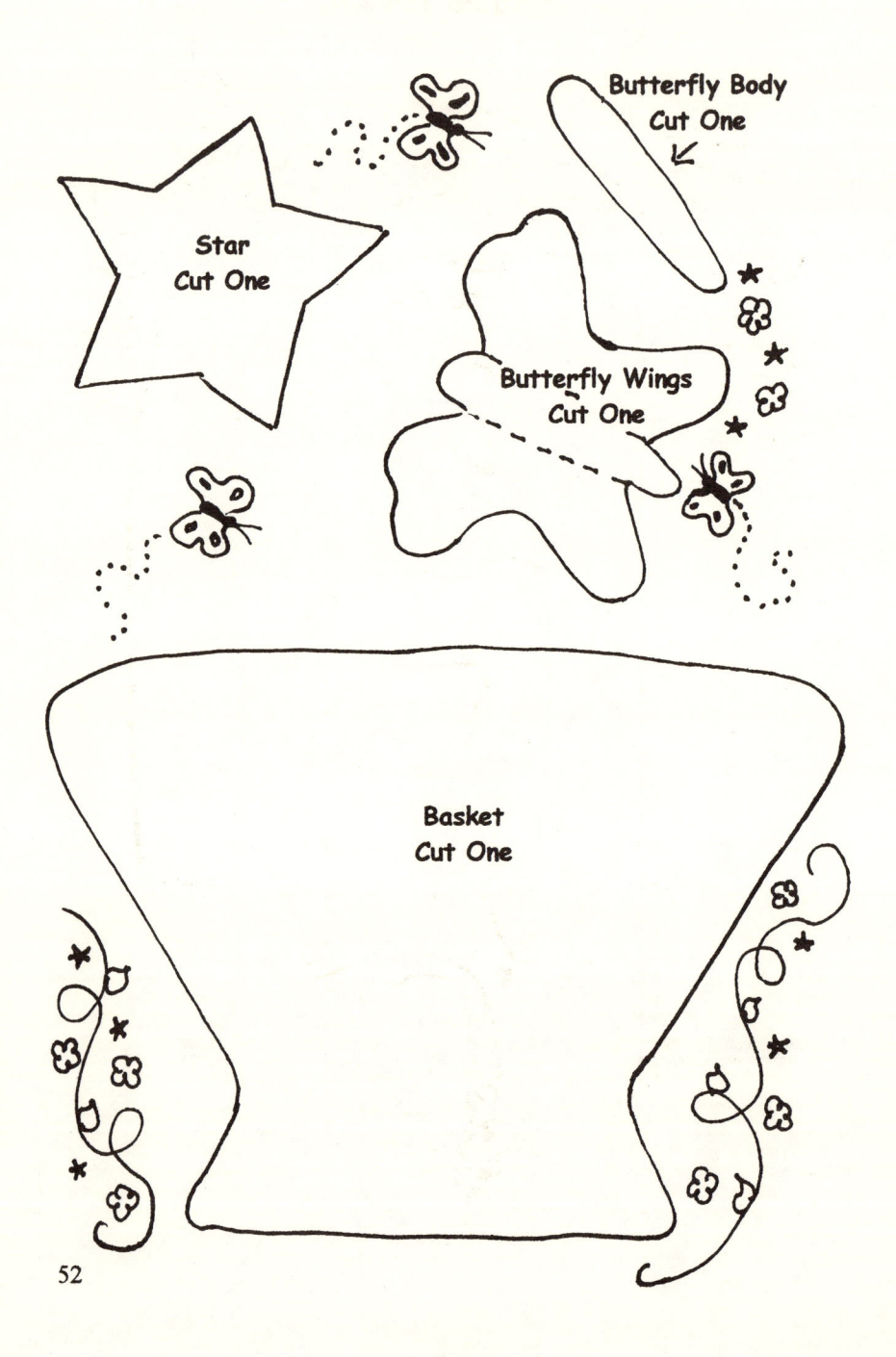

Butterfly Body
Cut One

Star
Cut One

Butterfly Wings
Cut One

Basket
Cut One

Mother's Day Basket
Remaining Pattern Pieces

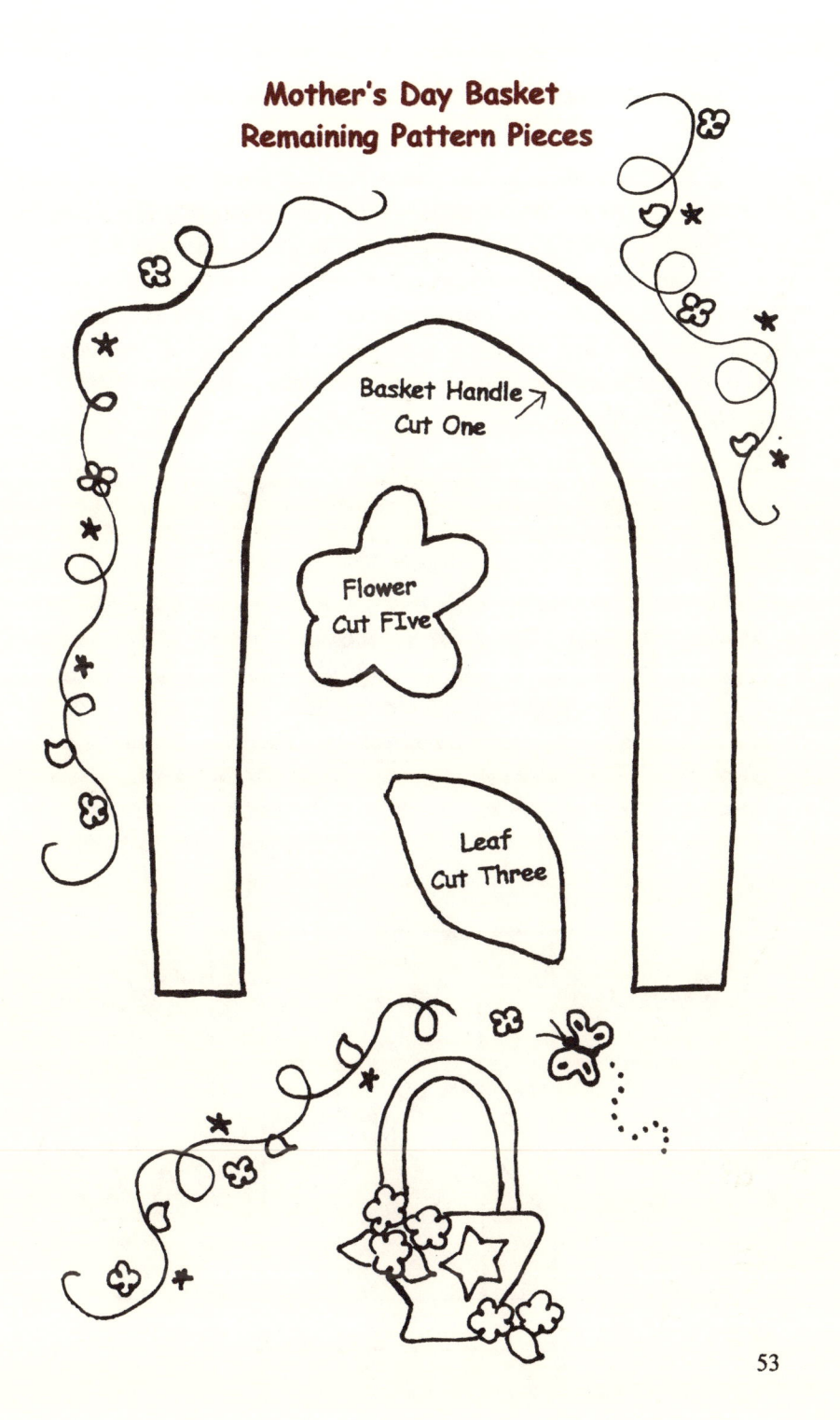

Basket Handle
Cut One

Flower
Cut Five

Leaf
Cut Three

Mother's Day Basket Instructions

Make the Double Star Block as instructed on page 16. Trace and cut pattern pieces as stated on each of the patterns. Cut each out of "fused" fabric. (See General Instructions on page 4.) Layer "fused" applique pieces on the star block center. (Refer often to full block drawing for placement ideas.) Iron in place. Blanket stitch around each applique piece. Chain stitch antennae and French knots at the end of each antennae. (See stitching Instructions on page 6.)

Wall Quilts:

Make a simple wall hanging with this block by adding a 2 1/2" border around the block. Cut a fabric back and batting 2 1/2" larger than the block top. Layer the batting between the block top and back. Pin all layers together. Quilt by hand or machine. Cut two strips binding 2" wide. Sew the strips together end to end. Fold the sewn strip lengthwise, wrong sides together and press. Sew the raw edges of the turned binding to the back and slip stitch in place. Sew "o" rings to the top back of the wall quilt to hang. This process can be used to create wall quilts with all of the blocks.

Father's Day Menu

Delectables for Dad

Grilled Ribs

Black Hills Baked Beans

Golden Corn Bread

Herb Roasted Salmon

Cottage Potato Salad

Spaghetti Supreme Salad

Creole Green Beans

Garlic Parmesan Rolls

Daddy's Oatmeal Cookies

King's Cake

**June Hints
And
Gone Fishin' Block of the Month**

Grilled Ribs

2 tbsp. salt
2 tbsp. white sugar
2 tbsp. brown sugar
2 tbsp. ground cumin
baby back pork ribs (3 lbs.)

2 tbsp. chili powder
2 tbsp. black pepper
4 tbsp. paprika

Mix dry ingredients together and rub the baby back ribs with the mixture. Grill slowly until completely done.
Serve the ribs with prepared bar-be-cue sauce if desired.

Black Hills Baked Beans

1/2 lb. ground beef or sausage
1/2 lb. bacon, browned and crumbled
3/4 cup onion, chopped
1 can pork and beans (16 oz.)
1 can kidney beans (16 oz.)

1 can butter beans (16 oz.)
1/2 cup brown sugar
1/2 cup white sugar
1 tsp. salt
1/2 cup catsup
1 tsp. dry mustard
2 tbsp. vinegar

Brown ground beef or sausage and onions until done. Mix browned meat and onion with remaining ingredients in a baking dish. Bake at 350° for 40 minutes.

Golden Corn Bread

1 cup yellow cornmeal
3/4 cup flour
1 tbsp. baking powder
1/2 tsp. sugar

1/4 tsp. salt
1 tbsp. melted butter
1 cup milk
1 egg

Preheat oven to 400°. Mix dry ingredients together. Whisk milk, melted butter and egg together. Stir in dry ingredients only until moistened. Spoon into a greased 8" square baking pan. Bake 20 minutes or until golden brown.

Herb Roasted Salmon

2 tbsp. olive oil
1/4 cup fresh orange juice
grated peel of one orange
2 tsp. tarragon

1 tbsp. crushed garlic
salt and pepper to taste
4 salmon steaks

Mix marinade: Combine olive oil, orange juice, orange peel, garlic, tarragon, salt and pepper. Add salmon to marinade for 1 hour at room temperature. Turn over twice to completely marinade. Preheat oven to 450°. Place salmon in an oven-proof dish and pour marinade on top. Bake 7 to eight minutes. Turn and bake 7 to 8 minutes more. Fish should flake easily when tested with a fork.

**Any Man Can Be A Father.
It Takes Someone Special
To Be A Dad.**

Cottage Potato Salad

5 large potatoes
1 large onion
3 hard boiled eggs
2 small sweet pickles
3/4 cup Kraft Miracle Whip salad dressing
1 tbsp. yellow mustard
1/4 cup sugar

Peel and boil the potatoes until fork tender. Cool and dice the potatoes. Dice onion, eggs and pickles. Mix the potatoes, onions, pickles and eggs together. Combine the salad dressing, mustard and sugar. Stir into the potato mixture and chill.

Spaghetti Supreme Salad

1 lb. spaghetti
1 bottle Italian salad dressing (8 oz.)
3 chopped ripe tomatoes
1 chopped green pepper

Cook and cool the spaghetti. Mix the remaining ingredients together and pour over the cooled spaghetti. (Add chopped onion and olives if desired.) Refrigerate overnight.

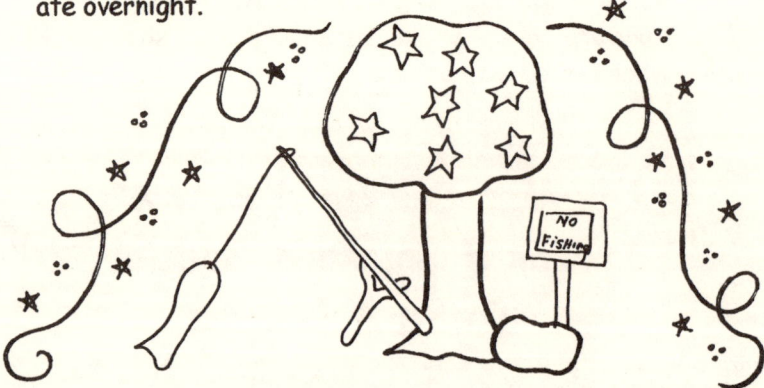

Creole Green Beans

2 lbs. fresh green beans
1/4 cup butter
1/2 cup chopped onions
4 chopped green onions
2 cloves garlic, minced
1 tsp. Creole seasoning
pepper
1/2 tsp. dill

Place green beans in a medium sauce pan and cover with water. Bring to a boil and reduce heat. Simmer for 10 minutes. Drain. Cover with ice water. Drain and set aside. Place butter and onion in a small fry pan. Sauté until onion is soft. Add remaining ingredients. Sauté for 2 minutes. Add beans and cook until thoroughly heated.

Garlic Parmesan Rolls

1 package frozen bread rolls
parmesan cheese
1 tsp. garlic powder
1/2 cup melted butter
 or margarine

Mix garlic powder with 1/2 cup of parmesan cheese. Roll frozen rolls in melted butter and then the cheese mixture. Place the rolls on a greased baking sheet. Cover and let rise until doubled. Bake at 375° for 10 to 15 minutes or until golden brown. Pour cheese mixture into the remaining melted butter. Warm leftover butter mixture and drizzle over the warm rolls

Daddy's Oatmeal Cookies

1/2 cup butter, softened
1/2 cup shortening
1 1/2 cups packed brown sugar
1/2 cup sugar
2 eggs
2 tsp. vanilla
2 tbsp. milk
2 1/2 tsp. cinnamon

2 cups flour
1 1/2 tsp. baking soda
1/2 tsp. salt
2 1/2 cups uncooked
   quick oatmeal
12 oz. chocolate chips
1/3 cup chopped almonds
1/3 cup chopped pecans
   (or nuts of your choice)

Preheat oven to 375°. Cream butter, shortening, brown sugar, white sugar and eggs together in a large bowl. Add milk, vanilla and cinnamon. Mix well. Stir in dry ingredients. Bake for 9 – 10 minutes for chewy cookies. Bake 12- 13 minutes for a crunchy cookie. Let cool one minute before removing from cookie sheet. Bake only one sheet of cookies at a time for best results.

King's Cake

1 pkg. chocolate with
   pudding cake mix
1 package instant
   chocolate pudding (4 oz.)
3/4 cup sour cream
1/2 cup vegetable oil
1/2 cup water

1/4 cup mayonnaise
4 eggs
3 tbsp. Amaretto liqueur
1 tbsp. almond extract
1 cup chocolate chips

Topping: powdered sugar

Preheat oven to 350°. Combine cake mix and pudding mix. Add sour cream, vegetable oil, water and mayonnaise. Stir until smooth. Fold in remaining ingredients. Pour into a greased and floured bundt pan. Bake for 50 to 55 minutes or until tests done with toothpick. (This mix makes up to 30 cupcakes if desired. Bake cupcakes 15-20 minutes or until tests done.) Sprinkle with powdered sugar.

Gone Fishin' Block of the Month
Applique Drawing

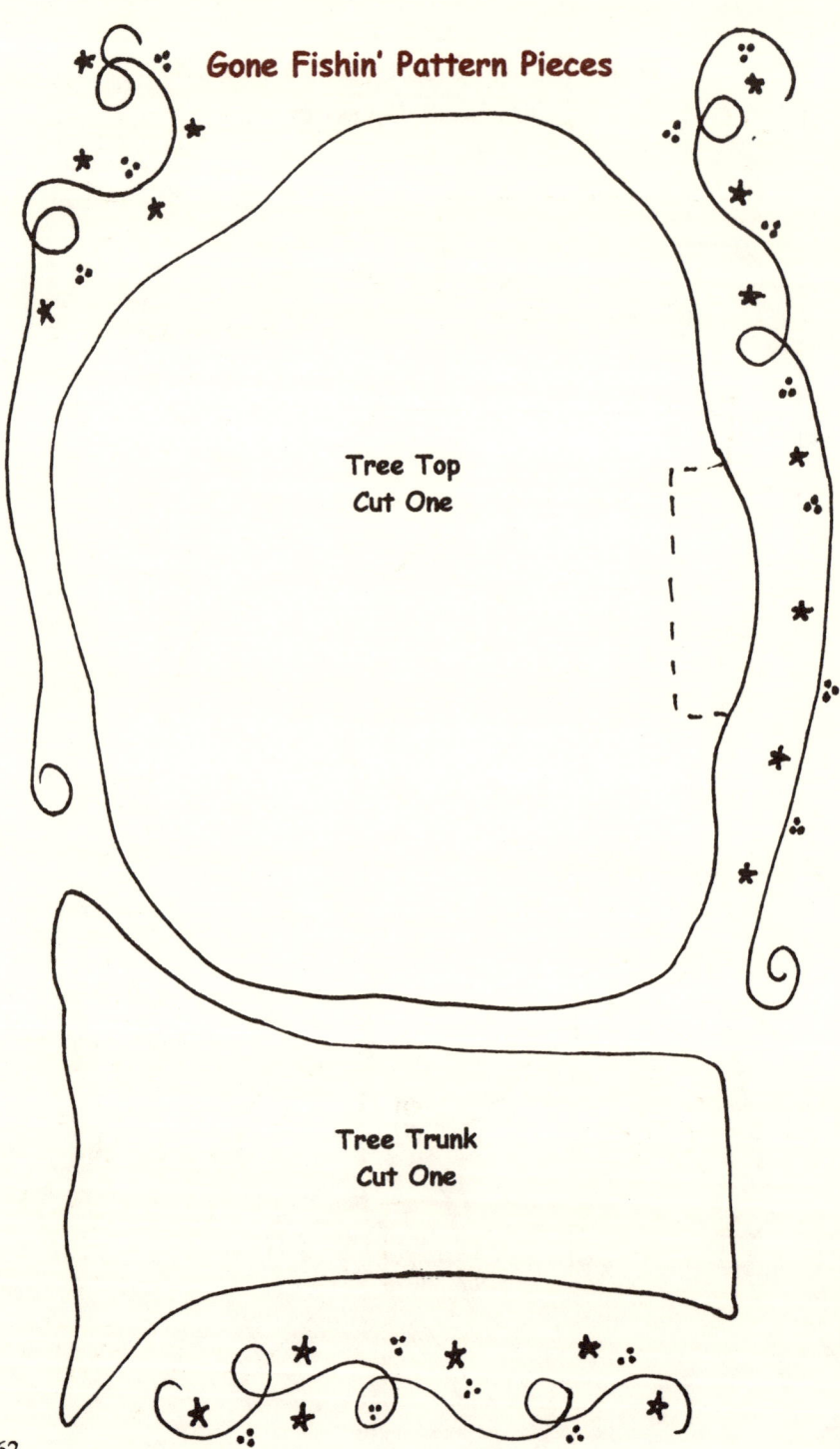

Gone Fishin' Pattern Pieces

Tree Top
Cut One

Tree Trunk
Cut One

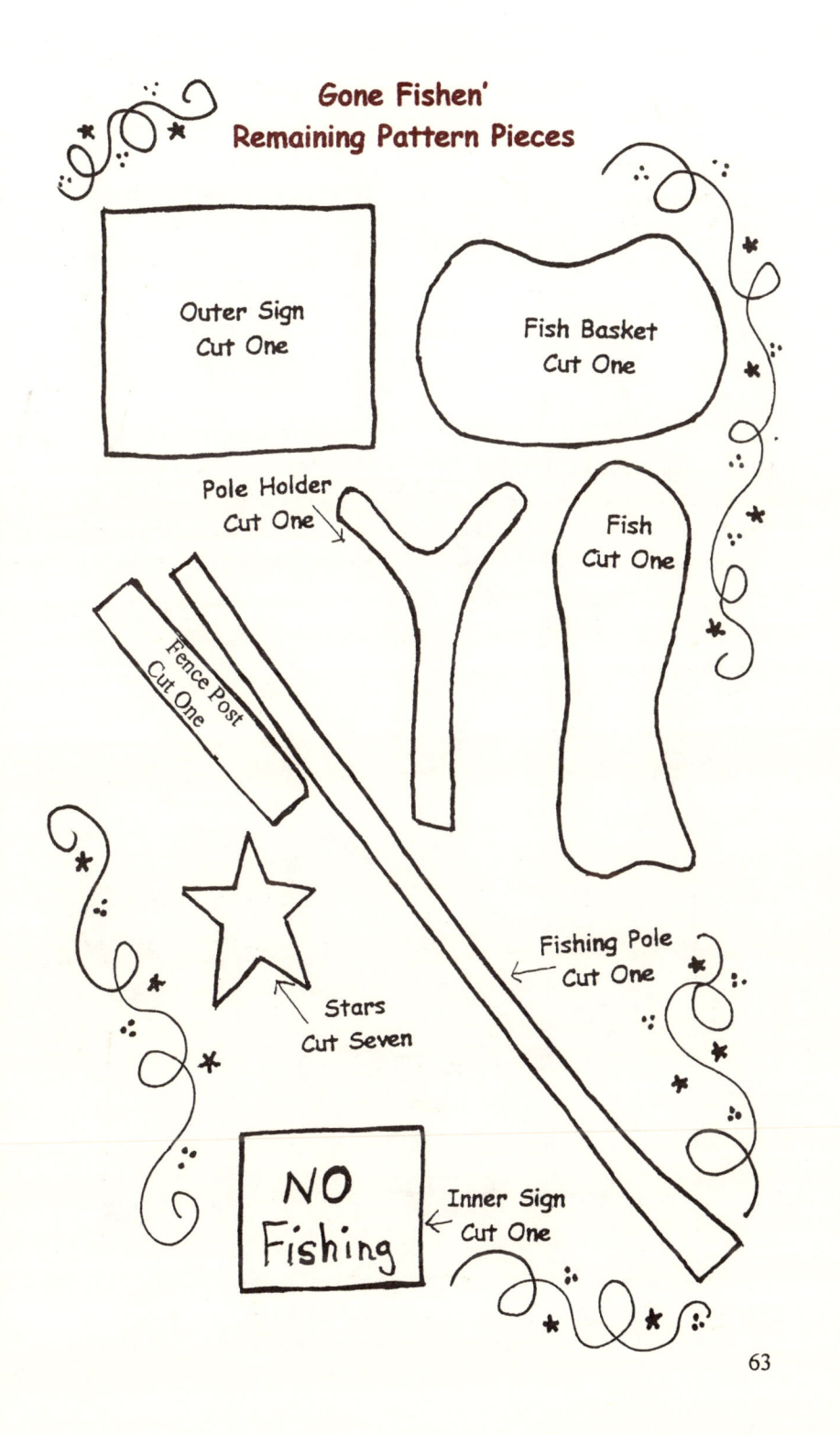

Gone Fishen'
Remaining Pattern Pieces

Outer Sign
Cut One

Fish Basket
Cut One

Pole Holder
Cut One

Fish
Cut One

Fence Post
Cut One

Stars
Cut Seven

Fishing Pole
Cut One

NO Fishing

Inner Sign
Cut One

Gone Fishin' Instructions:

Make the Double Star Block as instructed on page 16. Trace and cut pattern pieces as stated on each of the patterns. Cut each out of "fused" fabric. (See General Instructions on page 4.) Layer the "fused" applique pieces on the star block center. (Refer often to full block drawing for placement ideas.) Iron in place. Blanket stitch around each applique piece. Chain stitch the fish to the pole. Chain stitch the "No Fishing" on the center sign square. (See Stitching Instructions on page 6.)

Use this block design for the center of a lap top quilt. Simply keep adding borders made of blocks or strips until the quilt is the size you desire. Cut a backing and batting 4" larger than the quilt top. Sandwich the bat between the top and back of the quilt. Pin all three layers together every 4" – 6". Quilt. Add binding as stated in the small wall quilt description shown on page 54. This size of quilt is great to take fishing, camping, picnicking or just at home. Enjoy!

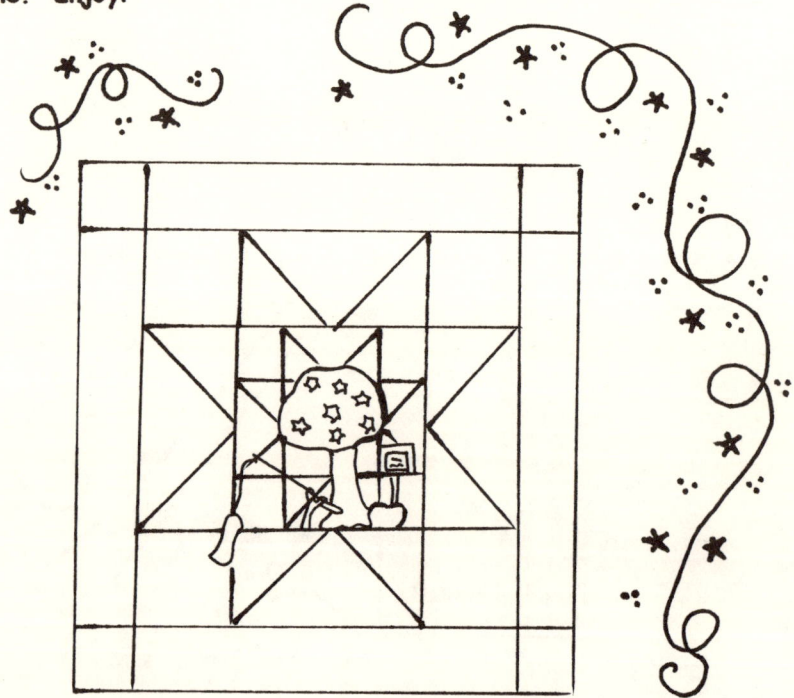

4th of July Menu

Patriotic Party

Summer Sloppy Joes

Summer Submarine Sandwiches

Chicken Grill

Summer Slices

Summer Salad

Frosted Fruit Salad

Frozen Champagne Salad

Summer Rum Slush

Summer Scrumptious Bars

Turtle Cookies

**Summer Hints and
Liberty Flag Block of the Month**

Summer Sloppy Joes

2 lbs. hamburger
 (cooked and drained)
1 can tomato soup or
 3/4 cup catsup and 1/4
 cup barbecue sauce
1/2 tbsp. vinegar
water if needed
hamburger buns

1/2 tsp. paprika
1/2 tsp. chili powder
1 tsp. brown sugar
1 tsp. Worcestershire sauce
1/2 tsp. onion salt
salt and pepper
1 tsp. yellow mustard

Combine all of the above ingredients in a large saucepan. Cook until thickened. Add water to make thinner if needed. Easy to make and fun to eat!

Summer Submarines

2 tsp. vinegar
4 tsp. salad oil
1/4 tsp. salt
1/4 tsp. pepper
1/4 tsp. Italian seasoning
1 loaf French bread
1 8 oz. package sliced
 bologna

1 package sliced salami (8 oz.)
1/2 package sliced Swiss
 cheese (8 oz.)
1 cup shredded lettuce
1/2 cucumber, thinly sliced
1 small tomato, thinly sliced
1 small onion, chopped

Mix vinegar, oil, salt, pepper and Italian seasoning together. Set aside. Slice bread horizontally in half. Arrange remaining ingredients on bottom half of bread. Top with vinegar mixture and remaining bread top. Cut sandwich crosswise into serving pieces and serve.

Chicken Grill

2 chicken breasts, boned skinned and halved
1/4 cup lime juice
3 garlic cloves, pressed
pepper
2 tbsp. honey
3 tbsp. butter

Place chicken breasts in a glass dish. Combine lime juice and garlic. Pour over the chicken. Pepper the chicken generously. Cover and let marinate about 45 minutes, turning a few times. Heat grill. Cook chicken over hot coals. Turn frequently until done. Mix honey and butter together. Serve chicken with sauce spooned over each piece.

Summer Slices

7 cups thinly sliced cucumbers
1 cup sliced onion
1 cup sliced green pepper
1 tbsp. salt
Combine all of the above and let set one hour. Drain well.
Dressing:
2 cups sugar
1 cup white vinegar
1 tbsp. celery seed
fresh dill

Bring the vinegar, sugar, dill and celery seed mixture to a boil. Pour over the cucumber mixture. Place all in a large jar and keep refrigerated until served.

Summer Salad

1/2 package elbow macaroni, cooked and drained (12 oz.)
3/4 cup celery
1/4 cup chopped onion
1/2 cup frozen peas
1/2 cup grated cheese
1 small tomato, chopped
1 cucumber, chopped
1/2 cup ripe olives, chopped

Dressing:
1 cup Miracle Whip salad dressing
salt and pepper to taste
1/4 cup milk
2 tbsp. sugar
1 tbsp. vinegar
1 tsp. yellow mustard

Mix the macaroni and vegetables together in a large salad bowl. In a small bowl mix all of the dressing ingredients together until smooth and creamy. Stir the dressing into the macaroni mixture. Refrigerate until served.

Frosted Fruit Salad

1 4 oz. package lemon gelatin
1 4 oz. package orange gelatin
2 cups hot water
1 small can crushed pineapple drained (save juice)
2 bananas, sliced
1 cup miniature marshmallows
1/2 cup sharp cheddar cheese shredded

1 egg beaten
2 Tbsp. Flour
2 Tbsp. butter
1/2 cup sugar
1 cup pineapple juice
1 4 oz. package softened cream cheese
1 cup whipped cream or Cool whip

Dissolve gelatins in hot water. Add cold water and let cool. Add pineapple, bananas and marshmallows. Pour into a 9" X 13" glass dish and chill until firm. To make topping, combine the egg, flour, margarine, sugar and pineapple juice in a small saucepan. Stir over low heat until thick. Cool and fold in cream cheese and whipped cream or cool whip. Spread over the top of chilled gelatin. Sprinkle with cheese. Cut into squares to serve.

Frozen Champagne Salad

1 package cream cheese, softened (8 oz.)
3/4 cup sugar
1 can crushed pineapple, juice and all (20 oz.)
1 package frozen strawberries, thawed (10 oz.)
2 bananas
1/3 cup nuts, chopped
1 carton Cool Whip (8 oz.)

Blend sugar and cream cheese. Add the pineapple, strawberries, sliced bananas, nuts and Cool Whip. Stir together. Freeze. Remove 30 minutes before serving.

Summer Rum Slush

2 cups rum
2 12 oz. cans frozen lemonade
1 liter lemon lime soda pop
2 lemonade cans of water
1/2 cup powdered sugar

Mix all of the ingredients in a plastic container. Place the lid on the container and freeze. Take out of the freezer 2 hours before serving. Stir while thawing. Serve in frosted containers.

Summer Scrumptious Bars

2 cups semi-sweet chocolate chips
1 package cream cheese, softened (8 oz.)
1 can evaporated milk (5.3 oz.)
1 cup chopped walnuts
1/2 tsp. vanilla

3 cups flour
1 1/2 cup sugar
1 tsp. baking powder
1 cup butter, softened
2 eggs

Combine chocolate chips, cream cheese and evaporated milk in a saucepan on low heat. Stir constantly until all ingredients are melted and smooth. Remove from heat. Stir in nuts and vanilla. Cool. In a large bowl combine flour, sugar, baking powder, butter and eggs. Mix until dough resembles coarse crumbs. Press half of the crumb mixture into a greased 9" X 13" baking pan. Spread cooled chocolate mixture over first layer. Sprinkle remaining crumbs over the top. Bake 35 - 40 minutes at 375°.

Turtle Cookies

1 cup + 1 tbsp. butter
2/3 cup cocoa
4 eggs
1/2 cup sugar
2 cups flour

Frosting:
1 1/2 cups powdered sugar
1/2 cup melted butter
2 tsp. cocoa
1 tsp. vanilla

Melt butter in a small saucepan. Add cocoa and sugar. Stir eggs and flour into cocoa mixture. Heat waffle iron. Put one heaping teaspoon of dough on each square on the waffle iron. Close lid and bake one minute. Frosting: Mix butter and vanilla with the powdered sugar and cocoa until smooth. Frost each waffle cookie with the frosting.

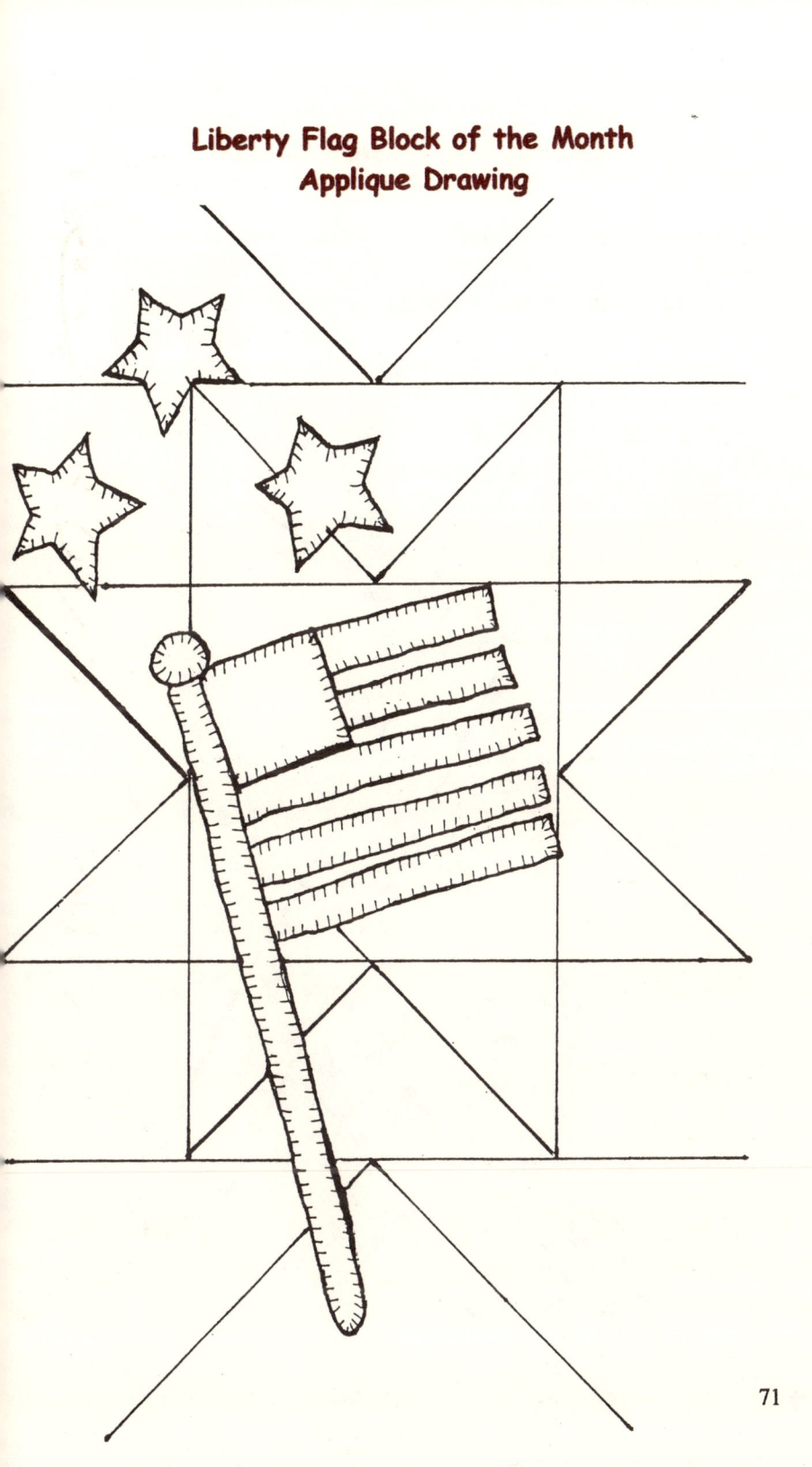

Liberty Flag Block of the Month
Applique Drawing

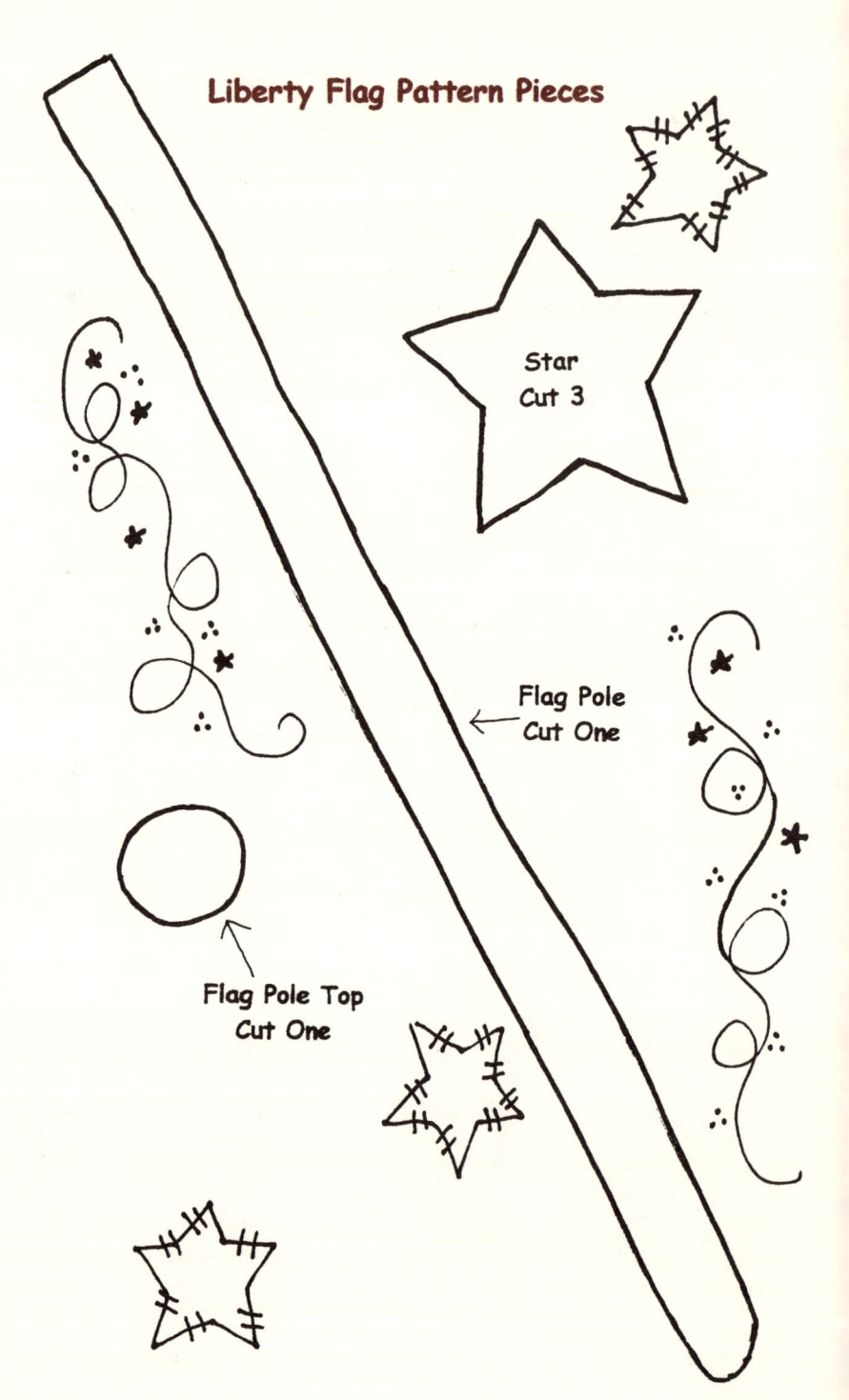

Liberty Flag Pattern Pieces

Star
Cut 3

Flag Pole
Cut One

Flag Pole Top
Cut One

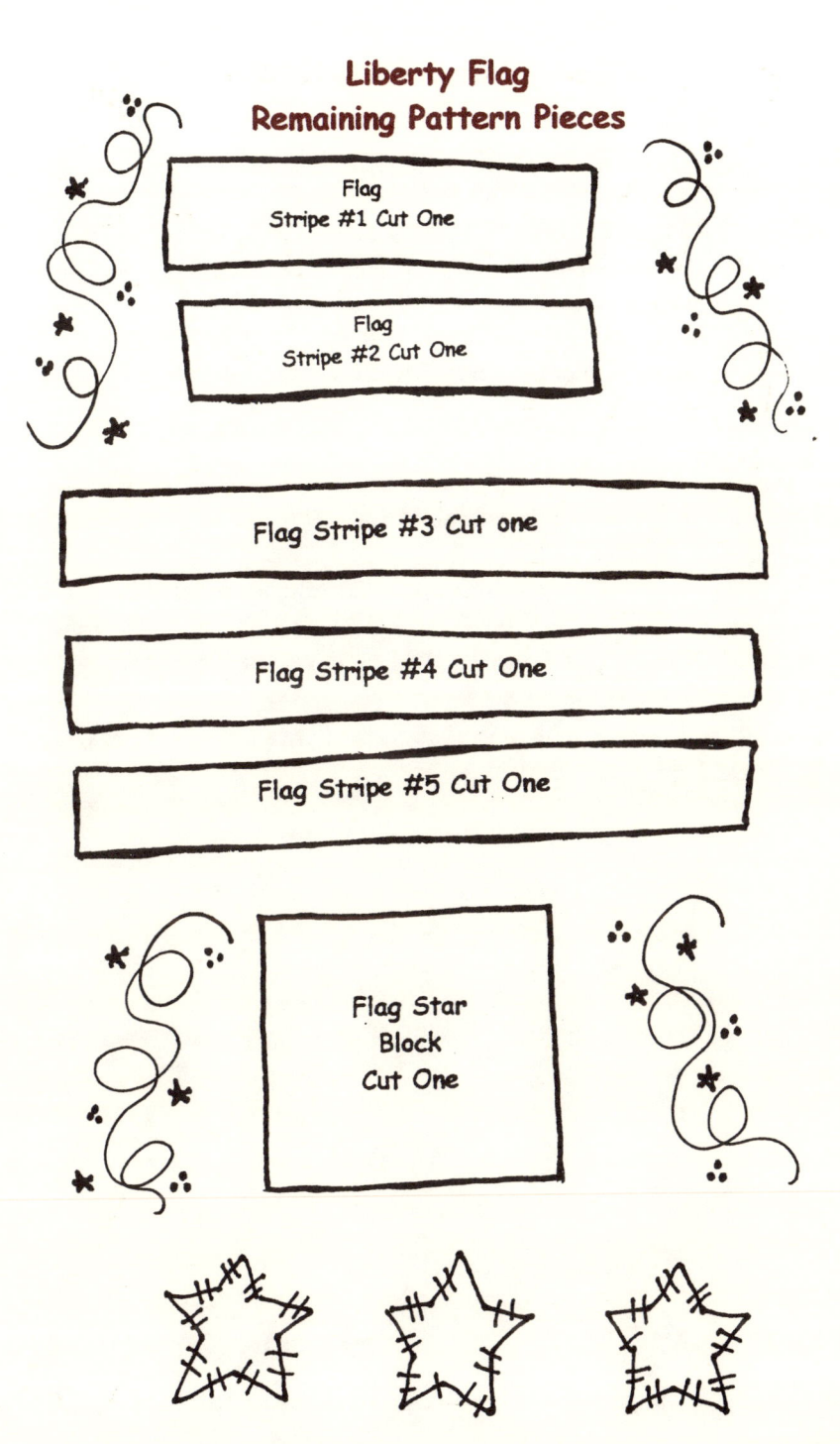

Liberty Flag
Remaining Pattern Pieces

Flag Stripe #1 Cut One

Flag Stripe #2 Cut One

Flag Stripe #3 Cut one

Flag Stripe #4 Cut One

Flag Stripe #5 Cut One

Flag Star Block Cut One

Liberty Flag Instructions

Make the Double Star Block as instructed on page 16. Trace and cut pattern pieces as stated on each of the patterns. (Check the direction of each piece before cutting.) Cut each out of "fused" fabric. (See General Instructions on page 4.) Layer "fused" applique pieces on the star block center. (Refer often to full block drawing for placement ideas.) Iron in place. Blanket stitch around each applique piece. (See Stitching Instructions on page 6.)

Iron the applique pieces from this block onto the corners of star fabric or a pre-made picnic tablecloth.

Create a Fourth of July centerpiece by arranging several half pint, pint and quart jars in the center of the table. Place a citronella candle in each jar. Light the candles to keep the bugs away.

Hang small red, white and blue Christmas lights on your trees, porch or deck to celebrate.

August Summer Menu
Fun In the Sun

South of the Border
Casserole

Easy Guacamole

Green Chile Sauce

Black Bean Salad

Apple Tortillas

Lime Delight

Old Fashioned Lemonade

Simple Slush

August Hints and
Sunflowers and Crow Block of the Month

South of the Border Casserole

1 lb. ground beef
1 small onion
1 can evaporated milk (5.3 oz)
1 pkg. dry enchilada spice mix
1 can cream of mushroom soup
   (10 oz.)
1 can chopped green chilies
   (4 oz.)
tortillas chips
3 cups shredded cheddar
   cheese
sour cream

Preheat oven to 350°. Brown ground beef and onion in a skillet, stirring until ground beef is crumbly. Drain. Stir in milk, enchilada spice mix, soup and green chilies. Layer chips, ground beef mixture and cheese 1/2 at a time in a 9" X 13" baking pan. Bake for 30 minutes. Serve with sour cream and guacamole if desired.

Easy Guacamole

2 large avocados, peeled
1 tbsp. lime juice
1/2 tsp. onion powder
1/2 tsp. coriander
1/2 tsp. garlic salt
tortilla chips

Mash avocados with the lime juice, onion powder, coriander and garlic salt. Serve with tortilla chips and other festive foods.

Stove Top Enchilada

1/2 lb. ground beef
1/4 cup chopped onion
2 medium potatoes, peeled and shredded
1 can chopped green chilies (4 oz.)
1/2 cup water
4 corn tortillas
shredded white cheese
green chili sauce (see following recipe)
lettuce
tomato

Brown the ground beef in a 10" nonstick skillet, stirring until crumbly. Drain. Add onion and potatoes. Cook until tender. Stir in green chilies and water. Cook until water evaporates. Heat the tortillas in the microwave or skillet to soften. Spoon mixture on tortillas and roll. Sprinkle cheese on top. Microwave until cheese melts. Spoon on the green chili sauce. Top with chopped lettuce and tomato. Makes two servings.

Green Chili Sauce

1 package frozen green chilies (10 oz.)
1 clove garlic, crushed
1/4 tsp. oregano
1/2 tsp. salt
dash coriander
3 tbsp. chicken bullion
6 cups water
3 tbsp. flour
3 tbsp. cornstarch
1 small tomato

Combine the cornstarch and flour in a small amount of water and stir to make a paste. Combine the green chilies, garlic, oregano, salt, coriander, bullion and 6 cups of water in a large saucepan. Slowly bring to a boil stirring constantly. Stir in the paste to thicken. Serve with enchiladas or other festive foods.

Sunflower Salad

12 slices crisp fried bacon, crumbled
2 cups broccoli florets
2 cups finely chopped red onion
1 cup sunflower seeds
1/2 cup raisins
1/2 cup sugar
2 tbsp. cider vinegar

Combine bacon, broccoli, red onion, sunflower seeds and raisins in a large bowl. Combine the mayonnaise, sugar and vinegar in a small bowl. Stir until smooth. Pour over the salad mixture. Stir to coat well. Chill covered until serving time.

Black Bean Salad

1 cup chopped tomato
1/4 cup chopped celery
1/4 cup chopped green onions
1/4 cup chopped fresh cilantro
1/4 cup lime juice
1/4 cup olive oil
salt to taste
1 cup cooked rice, cooled
pepper to taste
1/8 tsp. hot sauce
2 cloves garlic, crushed
2 cans black beans, rinsed and drained (15 oz.)

Combine the tomato, celery, green onions and cilantro in a medium bowl. Mix well. Stir in lime juice, olive oil, salt and pepper, hot pepper sauce and garlic. Combine the beans and rice in a large serving bowl. Fold in the tomato mixture. Chill uncovered for one hour or longer to blend flavors.

Apple Tortillas

1 can apple pie filling (21 oz.)
10 small soft flour tortillas
1 1/2 cups sugar
3/4 cup margarine
2 cups water
ice cream

Preheat oven to 350°. Spoon pie filling on each tortilla, dividing equally. Roll to close each tortilla. Place seam side down in a greased 9" X 13" baking dish. Combine sugar, margarine and water in a saucepan. Cook until the sugar is dissolved. Pour over the tortillas. Bake 20 minutes. Serve with ice cream.

Lime Delight

1 can crushed pineapple (8 oz.)
2 packages lime gelatin (3 oz.)
1 2/3 cups ginger ale
1 pint vanilla ice cream, softened
1/2 cup chopped nuts
whipped cream or whipped topping

Drain pineapple, reserving the juice. Combine the gelatin and one cup of the ginger ale in large saucepan. Cook over low heat. Stir in remaining 2/3 cup ginger ale and reserved pineapple juice. Pour into a large mixing bowl. Chill until thickened. Beat until light and fluffy. Add ice cream and fold in pineapple and nuts. Spoon into dessert dishes. Garnish with whipped cream or whipped topping.

Old Fashioned Lemonade

4 lemons
1 1/2 cups sugar

ice cubes
cold water

Slice the lemons as thin as possible. Placed sliced lemons and sugar in the bottom of a pitcher Stir until the sugar dissolves. Fill the pitcher with ice and cold water.

Simple Slush

2 cups apricot brandy
1 can pineapple juice (48 oz.)
1 can apricot nectar (48 oz.)
1 can frozen orange juice
 (16 oz.)

1 can frozen lemonade
 (16 oz.)
1 cup vodka or rum
 (if desired)
lemon lime soda
lemon and lime slices

Combine the apricot brandy, pineapple juice, apricot nectar, orange juice and lemonade in a container that can be frozen. Freeze. Mix two parts slush to one part lemon lime soda to serve. Garnish with lemon or lime slices.

**Sunflower and Crow Block of the Month
Applique Drawing**

Sunflower and Crow Pattern Pieces

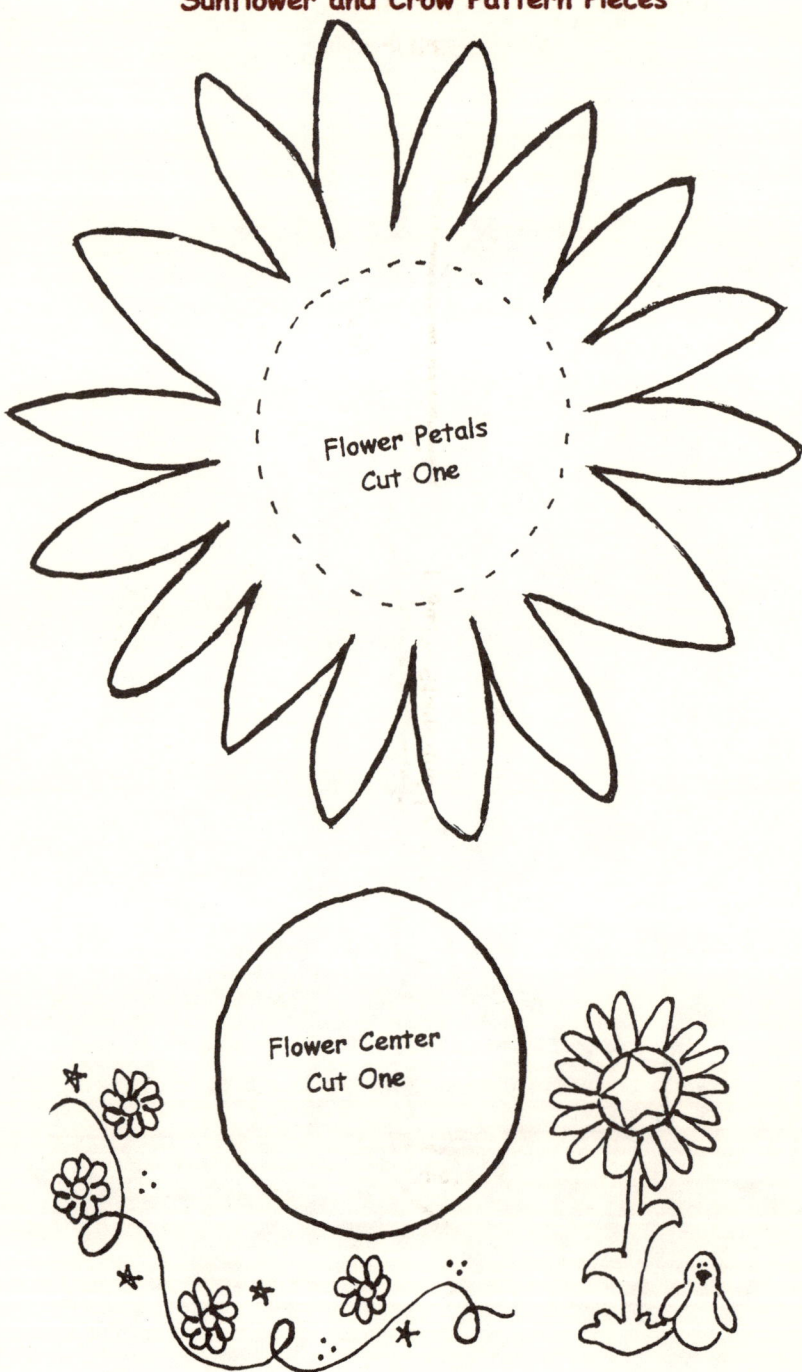

Flower Petals
Cut One

Flower Center
Cut One

Sunflower and Crow
Remaining Pattern Pieces Continued

Flower Stem and Leaves
Cut One

Flower Stem Bottom
Cut One

Star
Cut One

Sunflower and Crow
Pattern Pieces and Instructions:

Bird
Cut One

Bird Beak
Cut One

Bird Wings
Cut One Each

Make the Double Star Block as instructed on page 16. Trace and cut pattern pieces as stated on each of the patterns. (Check that each piece is going the right direction.) Cut each out of "fused" fabric. (See General Instructions on page 4.) Layer "fused" applique fabrics on the star block center. (Refer often to full block drawing for placement ideas.) Iron in place. Blanket stitch around each applique piece. Sew French knots on the bird's face for eyes. (See stitching Instructions on page 6.)

Iron this applique onto the center of a small brown paper bag. Place a vase inside the bag and tie a raffia bow around the top. (Be sure the applique is showing.) Fill the vase full of sunflowers and cattails for a great summer centerpiece.

Labor Day Menu

Leisure Time Lunch

Shrimp Salad

Caramel Apple Salad

Pasta Salad

Chicken Bake

Family Hash Browns

Apple Corn Bread

Zucchini Cake

Apple Sauce Bars

Surprise Pie

Labor Day Punch

**September Hints and
The Back to School Block of the Month**

Shrimp Salad

1 can black beans (15 oz.)
1 green bell pepper, chopped
1/2 cup celery, chopped
1/2 cup onion, chopped
2 tbsp. cilantro, chopped

2/3 cup salsa
1/4 cup lime juice
1 tbsp. vegetable oil
2 tbsp. honey
1 pound peeled cooked shrimp
lettuce

Combine the black beans, green pepper, celery, onion and cilantro in a large bowl and mix well. Add the salsa, lime juice, oil and honey. Toss to coat well. Chill covered for 8 hours. Stir in shrimp. Serve on a bed of lettuce.

Caramel Apple Crunch Salad

1 package instant butterscotch pudding (3 oz.)
1 cup crushed pineapple with juice
1 cup miniature marshmallows
3 cups chopped apples, unpeeled
1 cup dry roasted peanuts

Mix the pudding and the pineapple juice together. Stir in the remaining ingredients. Chill at least one hour before serving. This is a great tasting, long lasting salad.

Pasta Salad

1 1/2 cups elbow or shell macaroni
3/4 cup cheddar cheese
1/2 green bell pepper, chopped
1/3 cup chopped onion
1 celery stalk, chopped

1/4 cup sour cream
1/2 cup mayonnaise
2 tbsp. milk
1 tbsp. sugar
1 tsp. yellow mustard

Cook macaroni as stated on package. Drain and rinse with cold water. Drain again. In a large mixing bowl combine the macaroni, diced cheese, green pepper, onion and celery. Stir to combine.
Dressing: Mix the mayonnaise, sour cream, milk, sugar and mustard in a small bowl until creamy. Gently fold the dressing into the macaroni and vegetable mixture. Chill until served.

Chicken Bake

1/2 envelope Italian salad dressing mix
2 tbsp. melted butter
4 chicken breasts
1 can cream of chicken soup (10 oz.)

1 pkg. cream cheese, softened (4 oz.)
1/2 cup white wine
1 cup uncooked minute rice
parsley

Reserve 1/2 of the Italian dressing mix. Combine the remaining half of the mix and butter in a large skillet. Rinse the chicken and pat dry. Fry the chicken in the hot butter mixture until golden brown. Preheat the oven to 350°. Place chicken in a baking dish. Combine the soup, wine and cream cheese. Mix well and pour over chicken. Bake uncovered for 1 hour. Cook the rice. Serve the chicken over the cooked rice. Garnish with parsley.

Family Hash Browns

1 package hash browns, thawed (32 oz.)
1 can cream of chicken (10 oz.)
1 can cream of celery soup (10 oz.)
1 cup sour cream
1 cup cheddar cheese
1/2 cup chopped onion
salt and pepper to taste
butter or margarine
paprika to taste

Preheat oven to 350°. Mix potatoes, soups, sour cream, cheese and onion in a large bowl. Season to taste. Spoon into a greased 9" X 13" baking dish. Dot with butter and sprinkle with paprika. Bake 1 1/2 hours. Let set to cool 5 minutes before serving.

Apple Corn Bread

1/4 cup sugar
1 egg
2 tbsp. melted butter
salt
1 cup buttermilk
3/4 cup cornmeal
1 1/4 cups flour
2 cups chopped apple

Preheat oven to 450°. Combine sugar, egg, butter, salt, buttermilk, cornmeal, flour and apple in a bowl and mix well. Pour into a greased 9" X 13" baking pan. Bake for 25 to 30 minutes or until golden brown.

Zucchini Cake

1/2 cup shortening
1/2 cup vegetable oil
1 3/4 cups sugar
2 eggs
1 tsp. vanilla extract
1/2 cup sour milk
 (stir in 1/2 tsp. vinegar to sour milk)
1/4 cup baking cocoa
1 tsp. baking soda
1/2 tsp. salt
1/2 tsp. cinnamon
2 cups chopped zucchini
1/2 cup chocolate chips
1/2 cup chopped nuts

Preheat oven to 350°. Grease and flour a 9" X 13" baking pan. Cream shortening, oil and sugar in a mixing bowl. Add eggs, vanilla and sour milk. Mix until smooth. Fold in dry ingredients and add to the creamed mixture. Stir in zucchini, chocolate chips and nuts. Bake for 45 minutes or until the cake tests done.

Applesauce Bars

1 cup packed brown sugar
1 cup margarine, softened
2 eggs
1 cup applesauce
2 cups flour
1 tsp. cinnamon
1 tsp. baking soda
1/2 tsp. salt
1 cup raisins
1/3 cup brown sugar
1 cup butterscotch chips
3/4 cups chopped walnuts

Preheat oven to 350°. Cream brown sugar and margarine in a large mixing bowl until fluffy. Beat in eggs one at a time. Add applesauce and mix well. Stir in flour, cinnamon, baking soda and salt. Mix well. Stir in raisins. Spread in a greased and floured 10" X 15" baking pan. Mix remaining brown sugar, chips and walnuts together. Sprinkle over top. Bake 20 minutes. Cut into bars.

Surprise Pie

4 eggs
2 cups milk
3/4 cups sugar
1/2 cup flour
1/4 cup butter or
 margarine
dash of salt
1 tsp. vanilla
1 cup flaked coconut

Preheat oven to 350°. Combine eggs, milk, sugar, flour, butter, salt, vanilla and coconut in a blender. Process on high for 10 seconds. Pour into a buttered 10" pie plate. Bake 40 minutes. Cool before serving.

Labor Day Punch

1 can frozen lemonade
 (12 oz.)
1 can frozen orange juice
 (6 oz.)
1 quart cranberry-apple
 juice
2 quarts lemon lime
 soda

Combine the juices in a punch bowl, stirring until combined. Add the soda and mix well. Pour over an ice ring to chill.

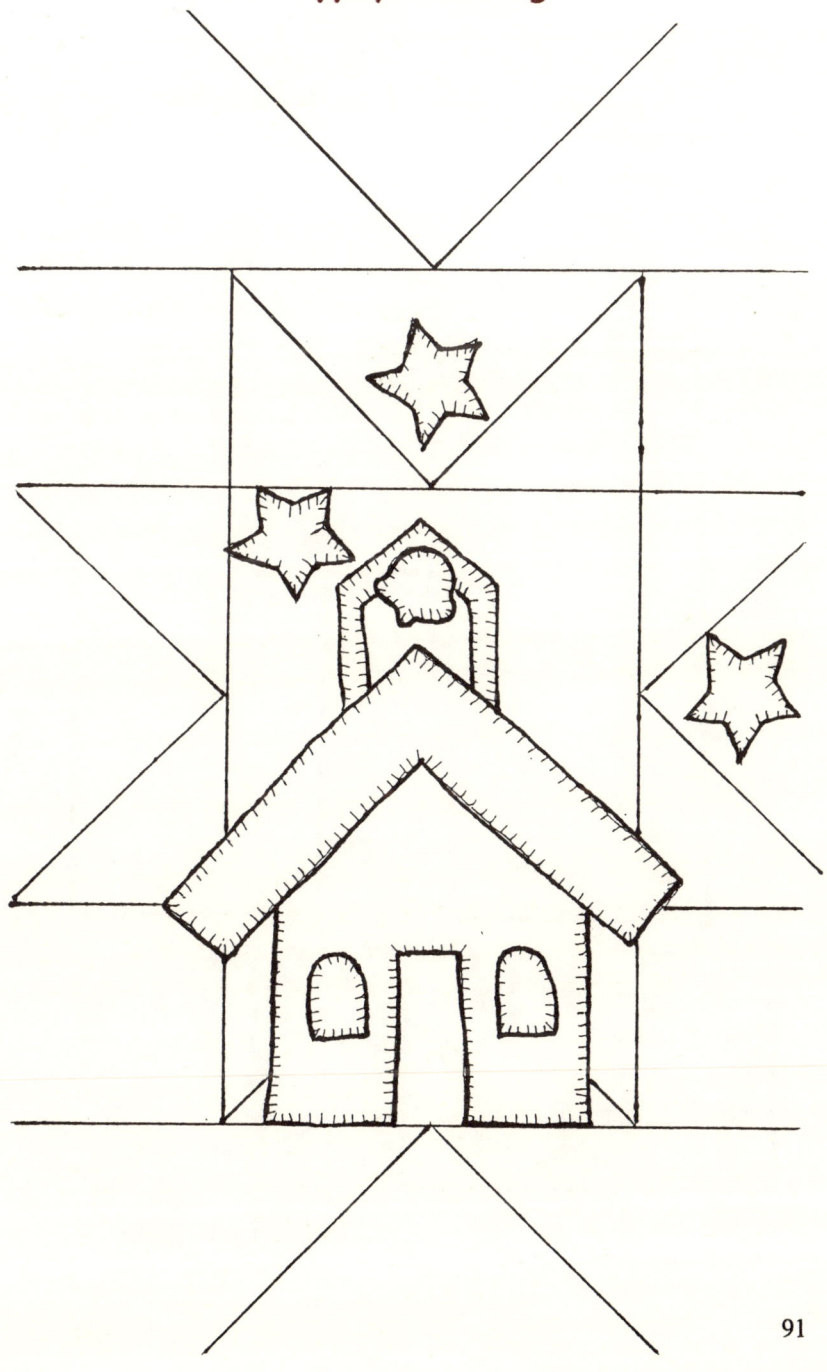

**Back to School Block of the Month
Applique Drawing**

Back to School Pattern Pieces

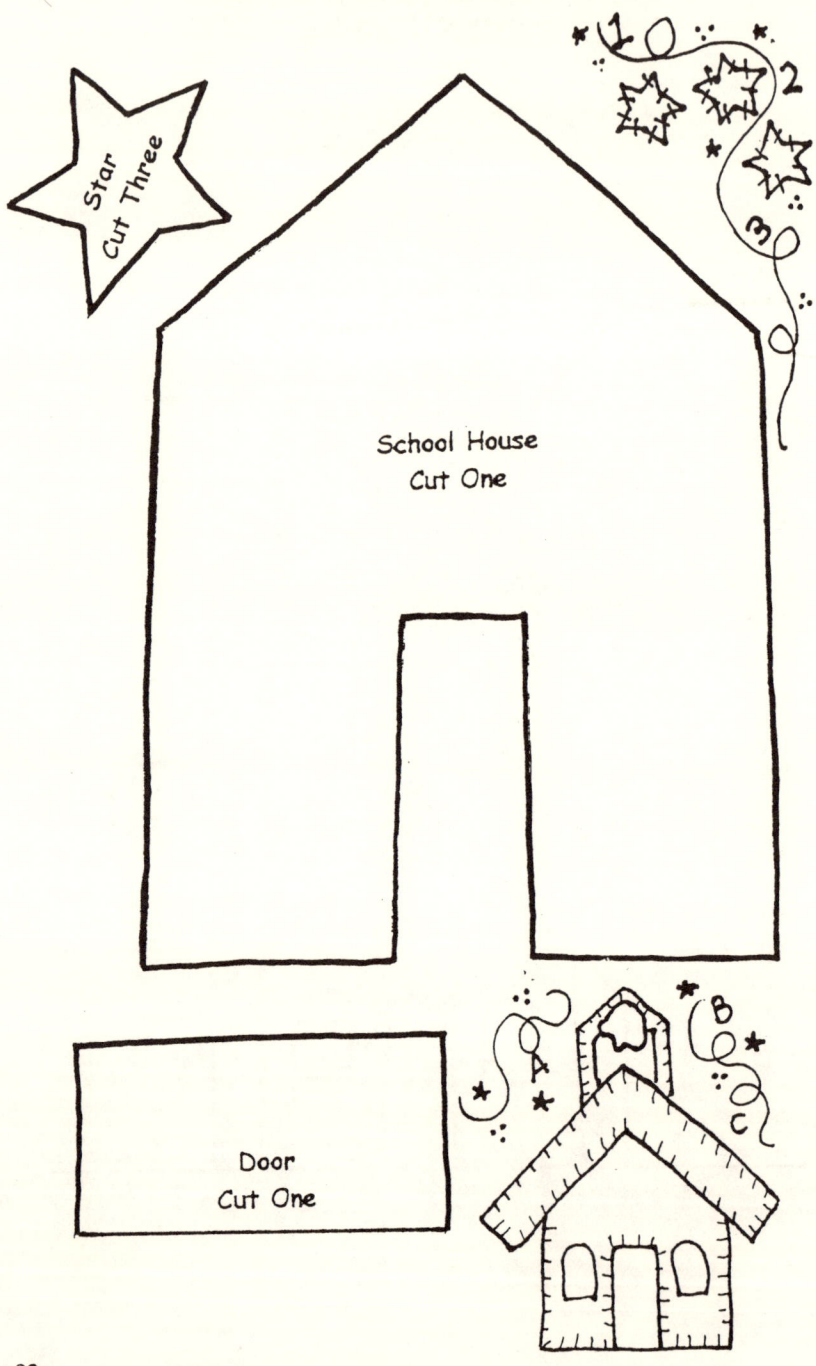

Star
Cut Three

School House
Cut One

Door
Cut One

Back to School
Remaining Pattern Pieces and Instructions:

Window Cut Two

Bell Tower Cut One

Bell Cut One

Bell Dong Cut One

School House Roof Cut One

Make the Double Star Block as instructed on page 16. Trace and cut pattern pieces as stated on each pattern. (Check that each piece is going the right direction.) Cut each out of "fused" fabric. (See General Instructions on page 4.) Layer "fused" applique fabrics on the star block center. (Refer often to full block drawing for placement ideas.) Iron in place. Blanket stitch around each applique piece.

Back to School Continued:

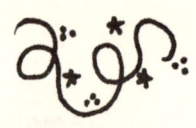

Use the Back to School Block to decorate Back to School tote bags, jumpers, skirts etc. Simply follow the instructions for all of the appliques and apply it to the project you are creating.

Notes:

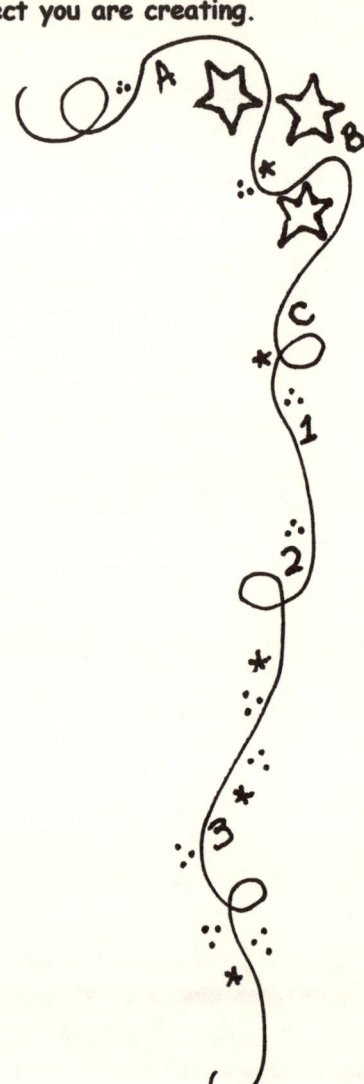

Halloween

A Ghoulish Good Time Menu

Apple Cheese Ball

Artichoke Dip
And Garlic French Bread

Mustard Dip

Sunflower Cheese Ball

Halloween Pate'

Cajun Spiced Pecans

Party Scramble

Caramel Fondue

Spiced Cider

**October Hints and
Pumpkin Surprise Block of the Month**

Apple Cheese Ball

1 package cream cheese, softened (8 oz.)
1 to 2 medium tart apples, finely chopped
3/4 cup finely chopped celery
1 tbsp. cinnamon sugar mixture

Combine the cream cheese, apples, nuts, celery and cinnamon sugar mixture in a medium bowl. Mix well and shape into a ball. Chill, covered until firm. Serve with crackers.

Artichoke Dip With French Bread

1 can artichoke hearts (14 oz.)
1 cup fat free mayonnaise
1 cup grated Parmesan cheese
1 tsp. lemon juice
1 tsp. garlic powder
1/2 cup sour cream
2 dashes Tabasco sauce
paprika
one loaf French bread

Preheat oven to 350°. Drain, rinse and chop the artichoke hearts. In a medium bowl stir together mayonnaise, parmesan cheese, lemon juice, garlic powder, sour cream and Tabasco sauce. Stir in the artichoke hearts. Spoon into a slightly greased 9" X 13" baking pan. Sprinkle with paprika. Bake 20 minutes. Serve hot with torn warm French bread.

Mustard Dip

1 cup mayonnaise or Miracle Whip salad dressing
1 cup sour cream
1 cup yellow mustard
1 envelope Ranch Salad Dressing mix
2 tsp. horseradish

Combine and mix all of the above ingredients until smooth. Chill until served. Serve with pretzels or crackers of your choice.

Sunflower Cheese Ball

1 1/2 cups salted, roasted sunflower seeds
1 package cream cheese, softened (8 oz.)
3 oz. bleu cheese, crumbled
2 tbsp. sugar
1 tsp. instant chicken bullion
1/8 tsp. red pepper
nacho cheese tortilla chips

Combine 1 cup seeds and all of the remaining ingredients. Stir until smooth. Make a ball and roll the ball in the remaining sunflower seeds. Chill covered until ready to serve. Serve with the nacho cheese chips.

Halloween Pate'

8 oz. liverwurst at room temperature
1 package cream cheese, softened (8 oz.)
1 tbsp. chopped chives
1 tbsp. Worcestershire sauce
1/4 tsp. dry mustard
dash of Tabasco sauce
lettuce leaves
crackers of your choice

Mix all ingredients in a medium sized bowl until smooth. Spray a non-stick cooking spray in the bottom of a mold. Pour mixture in mold and chill for one hour or longer before removing. Serve on a bed of lettuce leaves with crackers of your choice.

Seasoned Oyster Crackers

1 1/2 cups butter flavored vegetable oil
1 envelope ranch salad dressing mix
pinch of garlic powder
pinch of onion salt
1 1/2 tbsp. dill weed
1 tbsp. lemon pepper
2 packages oyster crackers (12 oz.)

Preheat oven to 200°. Combine oil, dill weed, lemon pepper, salt, garlic powder and ranch salad dressing mix in a large bowl. Stir in oyster crackers, tossing to coat. Spread on a nonstick baking sheet. Bake 1 hour stirring every 15 minutes. Let stand until cool. Store in a tightly covered container.

Cajun Spiced Pecans

2 tbsp. melted margarine
1/4 tsp. garlic powder
1 tsp. cayenne powder
2 cups pecan halves

Pour a mixture of the margarine, garlic powder and cayenne over the pecans in a medium bowl, tossing to coat. Spread the pecans in a single layer in a microwave safe dish. Microwave on high for 2 to 2 1/2 minutes, stirring one to two times. Let stand until cool.

Spooky Party Scramble

1 package miniature butter crackers (10 oz.)
1 package miniature cheese crackers (10 oz.)
1 package miniature pretzels (10 oz.)
1 package oyster crackers (12 oz.)
1 package Chex cereal (10 oz.)
1 cup peanuts
1 cup pecans
1 envelope ranch salad dressing mix
1 tbsp. lemon pepper
1 tbsp. dill weed
1 cup vegetable oil

Combine crackers, cereal, pretzels, peanuts and pecans in a large bowl. Mix well. Add ranch dressing mix, lemon pepper and dill weed, stirring to coat. Pour in the oil. Stir again. Store in an airtight container. Let stand for 1 hour or longer.

Caramel Fondue

1/2 cup butter or margarine
2 cups packed light brown sugar
1 cup light corn syrup
2 tbsp. water

1 can sweetened condensed milk (14 oz.)
1 tsp. vanilla extract

Melt butter in a fondue pot or saucepan over low heat. Stir in brown sugar, corn syrup and water. Bring to a boil. Stir in condensed milk. Reduce heat and stir constantly until the mixture registers 230° on a candy thermometer. Stir in vanilla. Keep warm over low flame. Serve with apple slices or popcorn.

Spiced Cider

4 cups apple cider or apple juice
2 cups cranberry juice
1/4 cup sugar

1 6-inch cinnamon stick (broken into pieces)
20 whole cloves
1 tbsp. allspice

Place the first three ingredients in a crock pot. Place the cinnamon, cloves and allspice in a cloth bundle tied with string. Heat. Steep for ten minutes. Cool to drinking temperature and remove the spice bag. Serve hot.

Pumpkin Surprise Block of the Month
Applique Drawing

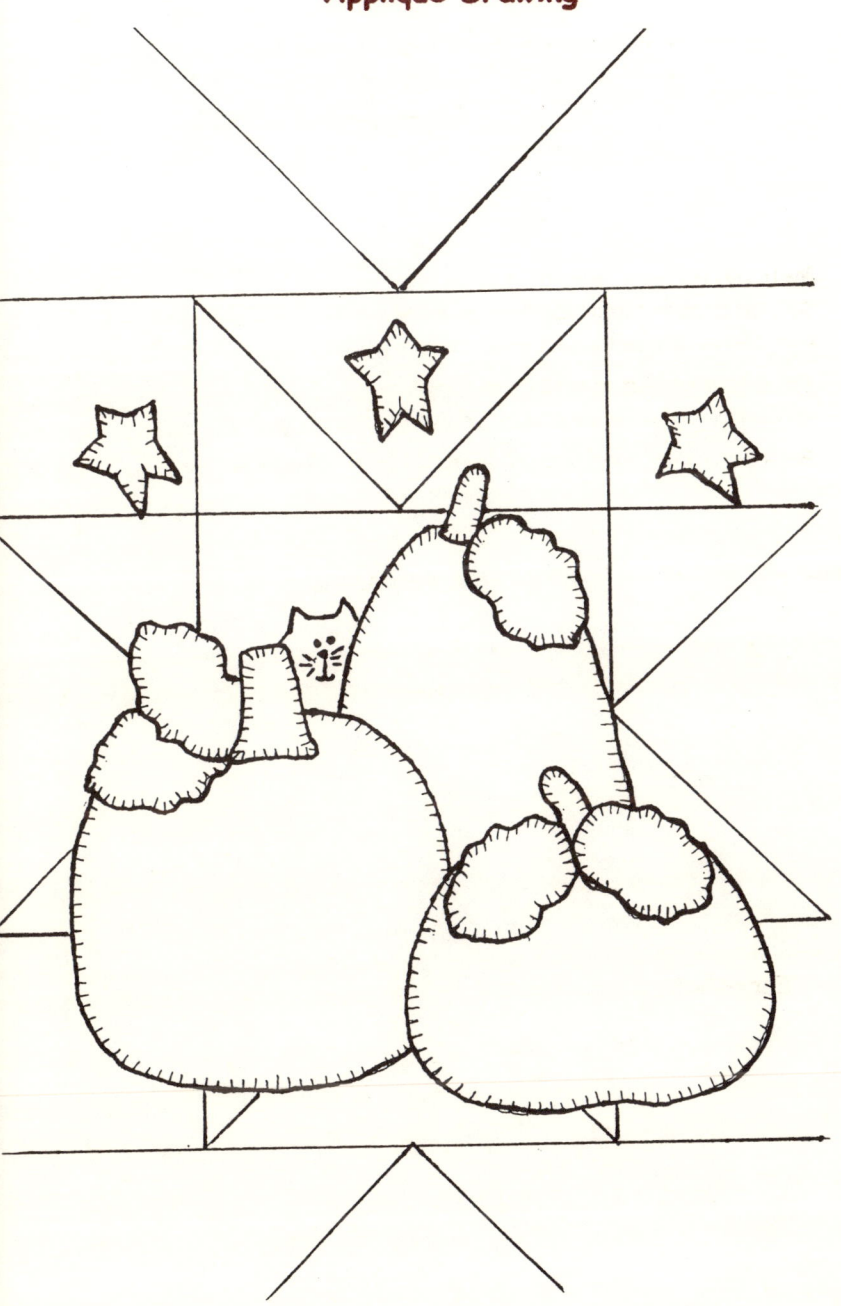

101

Pumpkin Surprise Pattern Pieces

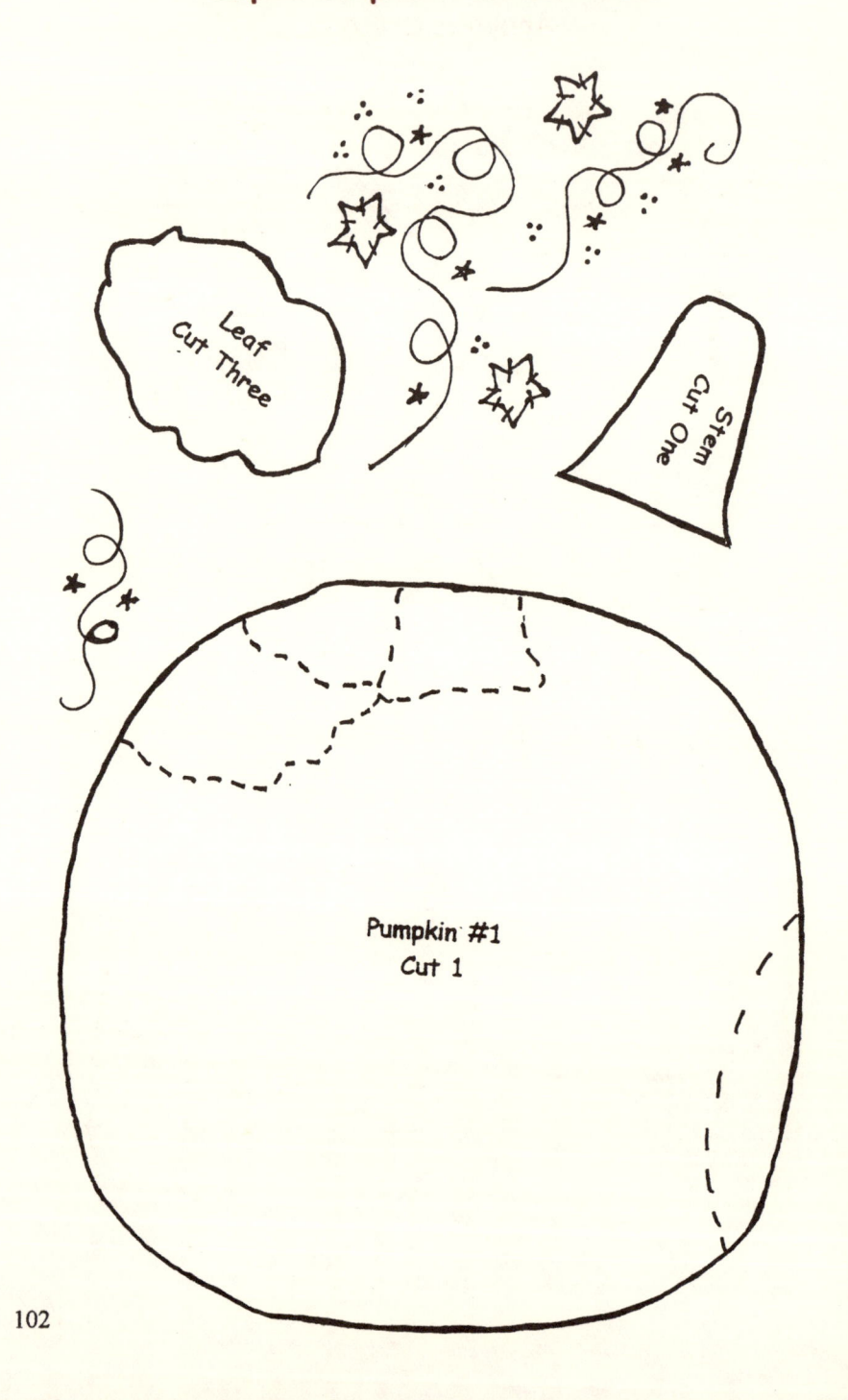

Leaf
Cut Three

Stem
Cut One

Pumpkin #1
Cut 1

Pumpkin Surprise
Pattern Pieces Continued

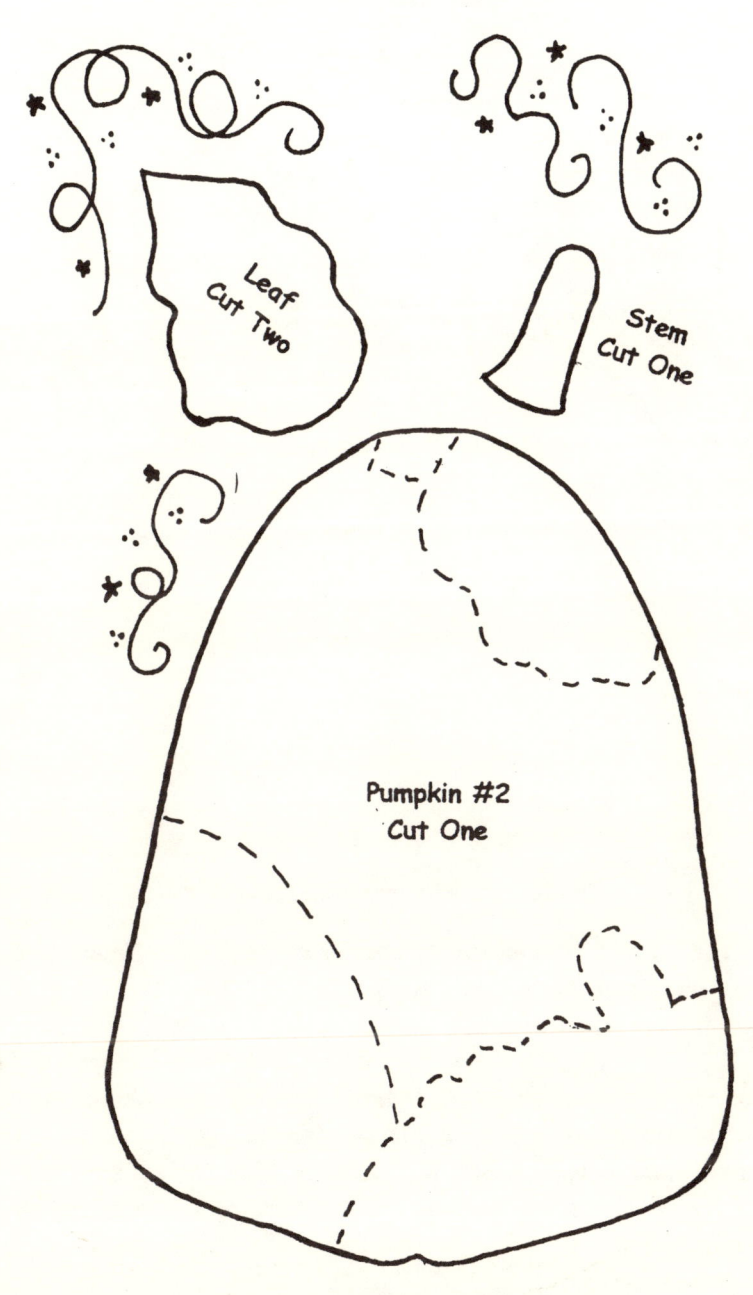

Leaf
Cut Two

Stem
Cut One

Pumpkin #2
Cut One

Pumpkin Surprise
Pattern Pieces Continued
And Instructions

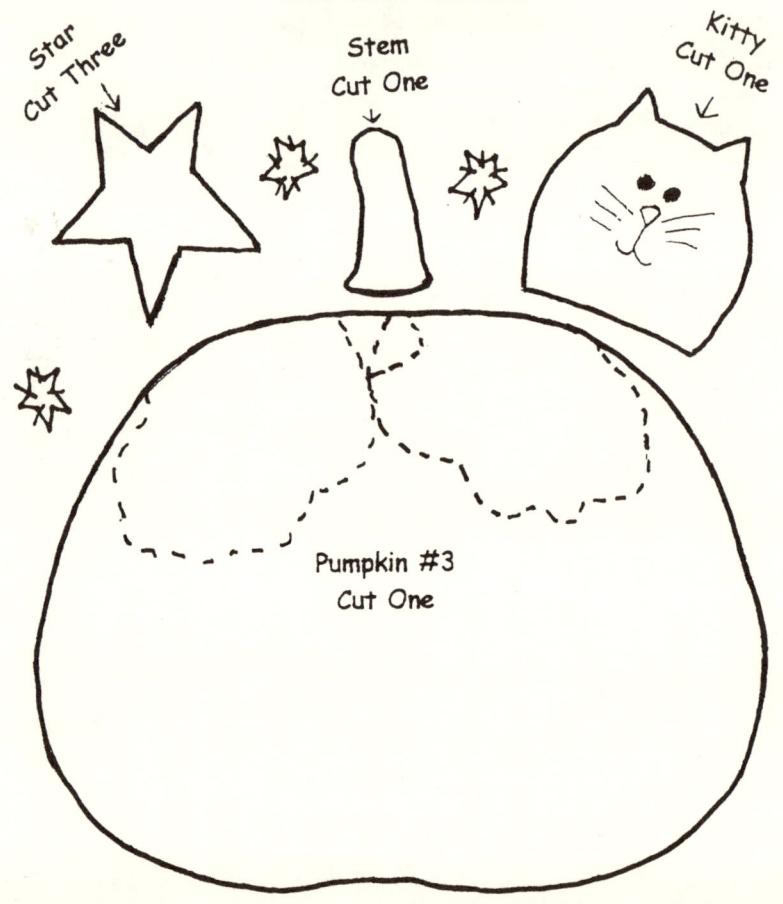

Star Cut Three

Stem Cut One

Kitty Cut One

Pumpkin #3 Cut One

Make the Double Star Block as stated on page 16. Trace and cut pattern pieces as stated on each pattern. (Check that each piece is going the right direction.) Cut each out of "fused" fabric. (See General Instructions on page 4.) Layer "fused" applique fabrics on the star block center. (Refer often to full block drawing for placement ideas.) Iron in place. Blanket stitch around each applique. Sew French knots on the kitty face for eyes. Chain stitch the whiskers and mouth, (See Stitching Instructions on page 6.)

Thanksgiving

Oh Thankful Hearts Menu

Family Fabulous Turkey

Seasoned Stuffing

Pilgrim Potatoes

Veggie Medley

Seven Layered Salad

Cranberry Crunch Salad

Cranberry Bread

Date Nut Bread

Pilgrim Pecan Pie

Pumpkin Surprise Pie

November Hints and
Thomas P. Turkey Block of the Month

Family Fabulous Turkey

1 turkey (10 - 12 lbs.)
1 quart water
1 apple
1 onion
3 stalks celery

Preheat oven to 350°. Place turkey, water, apple and cut celery stalks in a large roaster. Bake 3 to 4 hours or until meat thermometer reads 180° -185°.

(For a stuffing filled turkey bake the turkey 3 1/2 to 4 1/2 hours or until the meat thermometer reads 180° - 185°.)

Seasoned Stuffing

2 cups chopped onion
2 cups chopped celery
1 can mushrooms, chopped
1 cup butter or margarine, melted
12 to 13 cups dry bread cubes or croutons
1 tbsp. poultry seasoning
1 1/2 tbsp. ground sage
1 tsp. thyme
1 1/2 tsp. salt
1/2 tsp. pepper
2 eggs
3 1/2 to 5 cups chicken broth

Sauté onion, celery and mushrooms in butter until tender. Pour over bread cubes in a large bowl. Add seasonings and mix well. Add eggs and enough broth to moisten bread. Pack loosely into turkey body and around the outer edges of the turkey. Follow baking instructions as stated in the above recipe.

Pilgrim Potatoes

5 cups diced peeled potatoes
4 green onions
1 cup cottage cheese
1/2 cup sour cream
salt and pepper to taste
3/4 to 1 cup shredded cheddar cheese

Place potatoes and onions in a 2 1/2 quart microwave safe dish. Microwave on high for 10 – 11 minutes or until the potatoes fork tender. Combine the onions, cottage cheese, sour cream and salt and pepper with the potatoes stir to mix thoroughly. Microwave on high for 7 to 8 minutes stirring once. Sprinkle cheese on top. Microwave on high for 1 to 1 1/2 minutes or until cheese is melted. Let stand for a few minutes before serving.

Veggie Medley

2 tbsp. margarine or butter
1/2 lb. fresh asparagus, cut into 2" pieces
1/2 tsp. basil
salt and pepper to taste
1/2 lb. fresh mushrooms, sliced
1 medium tomato, cut into wedges

Microwave margarine on high in a 1 1/2 quart glass casserole for 30 seconds or until melted. Add the asparagus, basil, salt and pepper. Cover and microwave on high for 3 minutes. Add mushrooms and mix well. Place cover back on dish and microwave on high for 1 1/2 minutes. Let stand covered for 3 minutes before serving.

Seven Layer Salad

1 head lettuce, shredded
2 cups mushrooms, sliced
1 lb. cherry or Roma tomatoes
1 1/2 cups red onion rings

8 ounces grated cheddar cheese
1 lb. bacon, crisp fried and crumbled
1 package frozen peas, thawed (10 oz.)
mayonnaise

Layer lettuce, mushrooms, tomatoes, onion rings, cheese, bacon and peas in a large bowl or 9" X 13" glass pan. Spread mayonnaise over the top sealing to the edge. Chill, covered, overnight. Do not toss.

Cranberry Crunch Salad

3 packages cranberry gelatin (3 oz.)
1 cup boiling water
1 medium orange, peeled and chopped
1/2 cup chopped nuts

1 cup crushed pineapple
1 cup pineapple juice
1/2 package fresh cranberries, chopped (16 oz.)

Dissolve gelatin in boiling water in a medium sized bowl. Let stand until cool. Combine orange, pineapple, pineapple juice and cranberries. Pour the fruits into the gelatin and mix well. Pour into a 9" X 13" dish. Chill until set.

Cranberry Bread

1 1/2 cups sugar
1/2 cup margarine, softened
1 tsp. vanilla extract
2 eggs
1 carton sour cream (8 oz.)

2 cups flour
1/2 tsp. baking soda
1/2 tsp. salt
1 1/2 cups fresh cranberries, rinsed and drained

Preheat oven 350°. Cream sugar and margarine in a medium bowl. Beat until light and fluffy. Beat in vanilla and eggs. Add sour cream and beat well. Fold in flour, baking soda and salt. Mix well. Stir in cranberries. Pour into two greased and floured 5" X 9" loaf pans. Bake for 1 hour or until the bread tests done.

Date Nut Bread

4 eggs
1 cup sugar
1 1/2 cups vegetable oil
1 cup flour

3 cups chopped dates
4 cups pecan halves

Beat eggs, sugar and oil in a mixing bowl. Add flour and beat well. Stir in dates and pecans. Pour into a greased 5" X 9" loaf pan. Place in a cold oven. Bake at 300° for 1 1/2 to 2 hours or until done. Cool on a wire rack. Invert onto a serving plate.

Pilgrim Pecan Pie

22 butter crackers, crumbled
1 cup pecan halves
3 eggs whites
1 cup sugar
1 teaspoon vanilla
1 cup whipping cream, whipped

Toss cracker crumbs with pecans and set aside. Beat egg whites in a mixing bowl until soft peaks form. Add sugar and vanilla gradually. Fold in the pecan mixture. Pour into a greased 9" pie pan. Bake 30 minutes or until the top is slightly browned. Cool. Spread with the whipped cream.

Pumpkin Surprise Pie

1 package cream cheese, softened (8 oz.)
1/4 cup sugar
1 egg
1 (9-inch) graham cracker pie shell
1 1/4 cups canned pumpkin
1 cup evaporated milk
1/2 cup sugar
2 eggs
1 tsp. cinnamon
1/2 tsp. nutmeg
1/2 tsp. ginger
1/4 tsp. grated lemon peel

Preheat oven to 350°. Cream cream cheese, sugar and one egg in a mixing bowl until light and fluffy. Spread over bottom of pie shell. Chill well. Combine pumpkin, evaporated milk, 1/2 cup sugar, 2 eggs, cinnamon, nutmeg, ginger and lemon peel in a large mixing bowl. Beat until smooth. Spoon carefully over the cream cheese layer. Bake one hour. Cool. Top with whipped cream, chopped pecans and nutmeg if desired.

Thomas P. Turkey Block of the Month
Applique Drawing

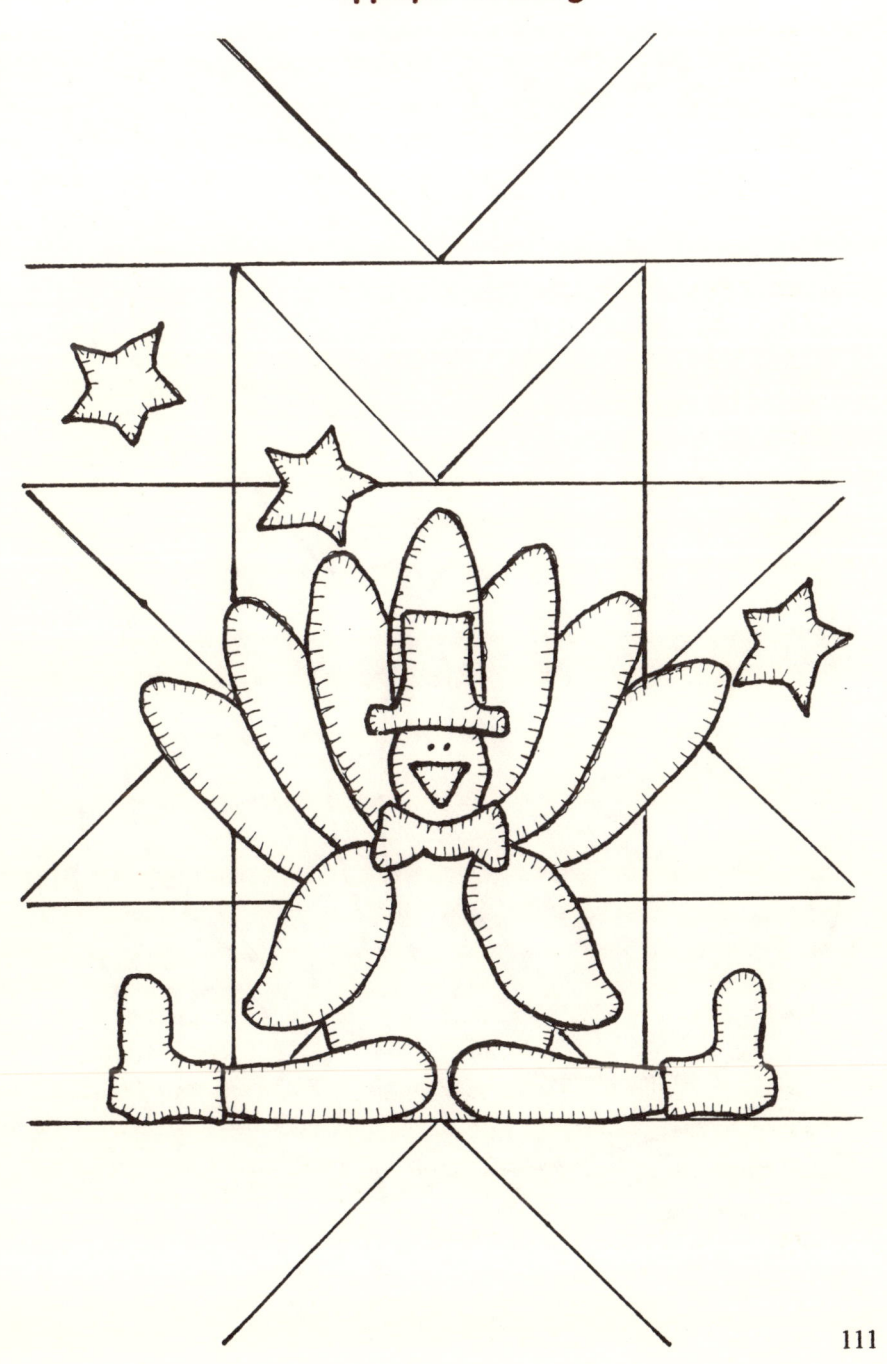

Thomas P. Turkey Pattern Pieces

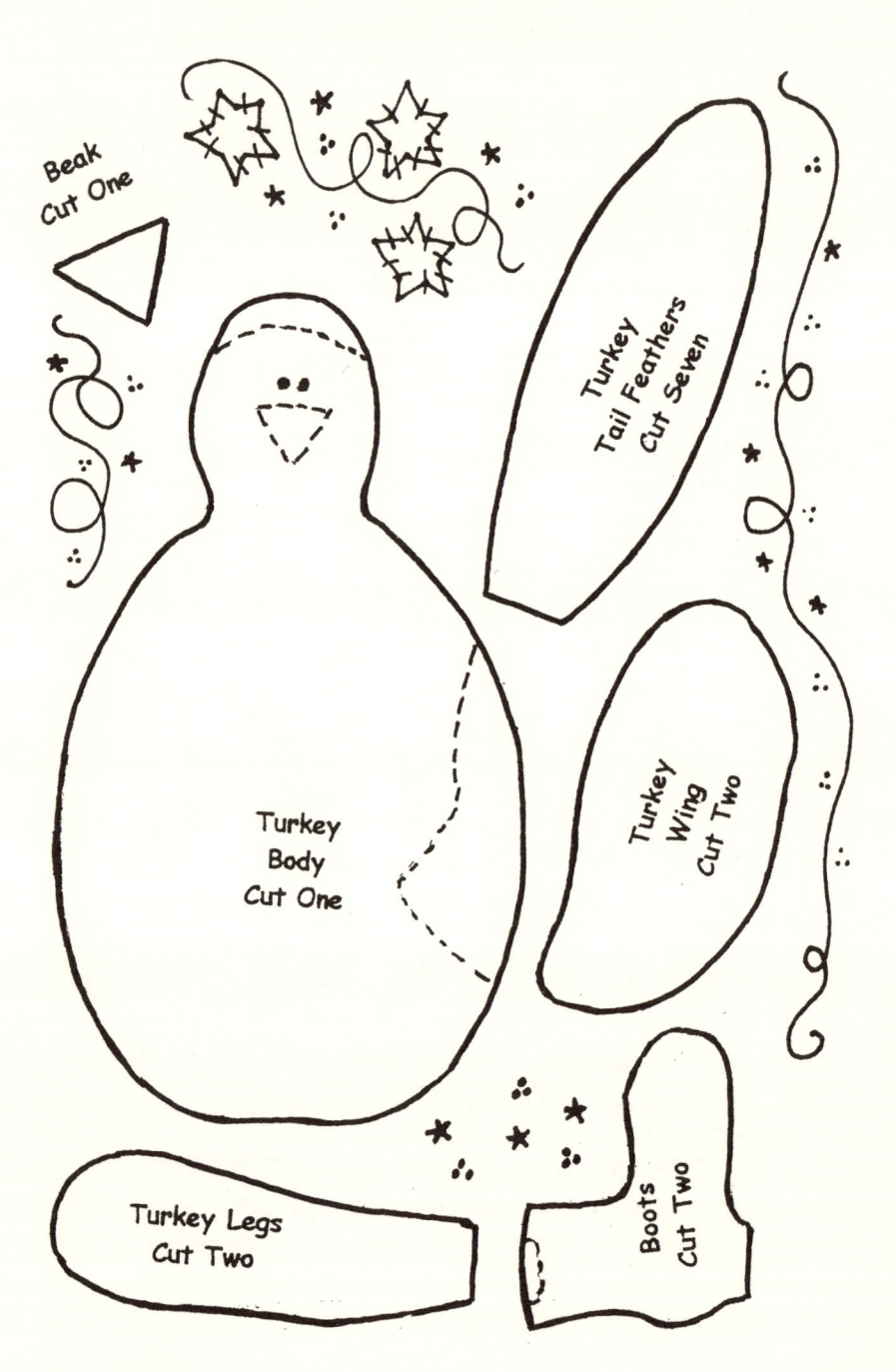

Beak Cut One

Turkey Tail Feathers Cut Seven

Turkey Body Cut One

Turkey Wing Cut Two

Turkey Legs Cut Two

Boots Cut Two

Thomas P. Turkey
Remaining Pattern Pieces and Instructions

Stars
Cut Three

Hat
Cut
One

Bow Tie
Cut One

Make the Double Star Block as instructed on page 16. Trace and cut pattern pieces as stated on each of the patterns. Check that each piece is going the right direction.) Cut each out of "fused" fabric. (See General Instructions on page 4.) layer "fused" applique fabrics on the star block center. (Refer often to full block drawing for placement ideas.) Iron in place. Blanket stitch around each applique. Sew French knots on the turkey face for eyes. (See Stitching Instructions on page 6.)

Thomas P. Turkey Continued:

Iron and stitch this applique to ready made place mats to make your Thanksgiving table look even more festive.

Fill an old tea kettle with water and a few drops of cinnamon and orange candy oils. Your entire house will smell warm and cozy.

Invite friends to bring their leftovers over and have a potluck.

Notes:

Christmas
A Festive Feast Menu

Oh Heavenly Ham

Twice Baked Potato Casserole

Red Cabbage and Apples

Seasonal Scalloped Corn

Rainbow Salad

Holiday Bread

Bread Pudding With Rum Sauce

Festive Fudge

Divine Divinity

Egg Nog Punch

December Hints and
Santa On His Way Block of the Month

Oh Heavenly Ham

1 cooked ham (2 lb.)
1 can pineapple chunks (8 oz.)
1/2 cup brown sugar
1 tbsp. cornstarch
1/2 tsp. ground cloves
1/2 tsp. ground nutmeg

1/3 cup orange juice
juice from pineapple
2 tbsp. water

Trim fat from ham. Slice top of ham with cross cuts about 1/2" deep. Place ham in a baking pan. Bake at 350° for 30 minutes. Remove from oven. Pour juice from pineapple and orange juice in a small sauce pan. Mix cornstarch and water together, forming a paste. Bring juices to a boil and stir in the cornstarch paste. Stir constantly until thickened. Stir in the remaining ingredients. Pour sauce over ham to serve.

Seasonal Scalloped Corn

1 can cream style corn (8 oz.)
1 can whole kernel corn (8 oz.)
1/2 cup chopped onion
1/4 cup chopped green bell pepper

2 tbsp. margarine or butter
1 beaten eggs
1/2 cup milk
1/2 cup crushed crackers
salt and pepper to taste

Drain the can of whole kernel corn. Pour both types of corn into a medium ovenproof bowl. Stir in beaten eggs, onion, green pepper and margarine or butter. Add milk, crackers, salt and pepper. Stir thoroughly. Bake in a 350° oven for 30 to 45 minutes or until the top is golden brown.

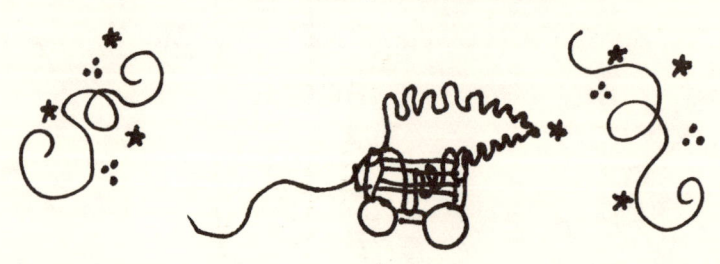

Twice Baked Potato Casserole

6 baking potatoes, baked
1 large sweet onion, chopped
1 green bell pepper, chopped
6 slices of bacon, cut small
salt and pepper
1/2 cup milk
1/4 cup butter
1 cup shredded cheddar cheese

Scoop baked potatoes out of skins into a large casserole bowl. Mash. Add enough melted butter and milk to make potatoes fluffy. Cook onion and green pepper with bacon pieces until bacon is crisp fried. Drain off fat. Stir bacon, green pepper and onion into potatoes. Stir 3/4 cup of the cheese into potatoes. Sprinkle the top with the remaining cheese. Bake at 350° for one hour.

Red Cabbage & Apples

1/4 cup butter, melted
2 sweet onions, chopped
2 tsp. salt.
3/4 tsp. pepper
1/2 tsp. ground nutmeg
1 head cabbage, chopped
4 apples, peeled and chopped
1 can chicken broth (14 oz.)
3 tbsp. lemon juice
2 tbsp. apple cider vinegar

In a baking dish melt butter over medium heat. Stir in onions, salt, pepper and nutmeg. Cook until onions are tender. Add remaining ingredients and bring to a boil. Reduce heat to medium-low and simmer 25 to 30 minutes or until cabbage and apples are tender.

Rainbow Salad

2 packages lime gelatin (3 oz.)
2 packages lemon gelatin (3 oz.)
2 packages orange gelatin (3 oz.)
2 packages strawberry gelatin (3 oz.)
4 cans evaporated milk (5.3 oz.)

Dissolve 1 package lime gelatin in 1 cup boiling water. Add 2/3 cup cold water. Pour this first layer into a 9" X 13" glass baking dish or a large mold and let set. Dissolve another package of lime gelatin in 1 cup of boiling water, add 2/3 cup evaporated milk. Pour on top of first layer and set. Repeat this process for remaining layers until the mold is full. Adjusts well for any occasion and color scheme.

Holiday Bread

3 packages dry yeast
1/4 cup lukewarm water
1 cup milk, scalded, cooled
1 cup shortening
1 cup sugar
2 eggs, beaten

1 tsp. salt
1 tsp. cardamom
1 cup raisins
1 cup walnuts, chopped
7 cups flour

Soften yeast in water, add milk. Cream shortening and sugar. Stir in yeast and milk mixture. Add beaten eggs. Mix well. Fold in spices, raisins and walnuts. Stir in enough flour to make a stiff dough. Spread remaining flour on counter top and knead until dough is smooth. Place dough in a greased bowl. Cover and let rise until doubled. Punch down and form into five loaves. Place the loaves in greased loaf pans. Let rise until double. Brush the loaf tops with melted butter. Bake at 350° for 45 to 50 minutes or until golden brown.

Bread Pudding

2 cups hot milk
2 cups cubed bread
3 tbsp. butter, melted
2 eggs, beaten
1/2 cup honey

1/2 tsp. cinnamon
1 tsp. vanilla
1/4 tsp. salt
1 cup raisins

Add hot milk to bread, butter and honey. Let stand until cold. Stir in eggs, bread, cinnamon, vanilla, salt and raisins. Mix lightly. Pour into a greased 9" X 9" pan. Bake at 350° for 1 hour. Serve with whipped cream if desired.

Festive Fudge

4 1/2 cups sugar
1 can evaporated milk (5.3 oz.)
3 packages chocolate chips (6 oz.)
1 cup butter, melted

2 cups chopped walnuts
1/2 pound marshmallows
2 tsp. vanilla

Combine sugar and evaporated milk in a large heavy sauce pan. Bring to a rolling boil, stirring constantly. Remove from heat and stir in chocolate chips, butter, walnuts and marshmallows. Stir until chips and marshmallows are melted. Pour into a greased 9" X 13" pan. Cool and cut into 1" squares.

Divine Divinity

3 cups sugar
3/4 cup light corn syrup
1/2 cup hot water

2 egg whites
1 package raspberry gelatin
   (3 oz.)
1/2 cup chopped nuts

Pour syrup, sugar and water in a sauce pan. Bring to a boil and cook until the temperature reads 250° on a candy thermometer. Beat egg whites until foamy. Stir in the gelatin, continue beating until egg whites stand in peaks. Slowly add the hot syrup mixture until the candy holds its shape. Beat in the nuts. Drop by heaping teaspoons full onto waxed paper.

Egg Nog Punch

2 cartons egg nog (1 qt. cartons)
1/2 cup packed brown sugar
3 tbsp. instant coffee
1/2 tsp. cinnamon

1/2 tsp. nutmeg
1 cup Irish whiskey
1 quart coffee flavored
   ice cream

Combine egg nog, brown sugar, instant coffee and spices in a large bowl. Mix until smooth. Stir in Irish whiskey. Chill for 1 to 2 hours. Pour into a punch bowl. Top the punch with scoops of ice cream.

**Santa On His Way Block of the Month
Applique Drawing**

121

Santa On His Way Pattern Pieces

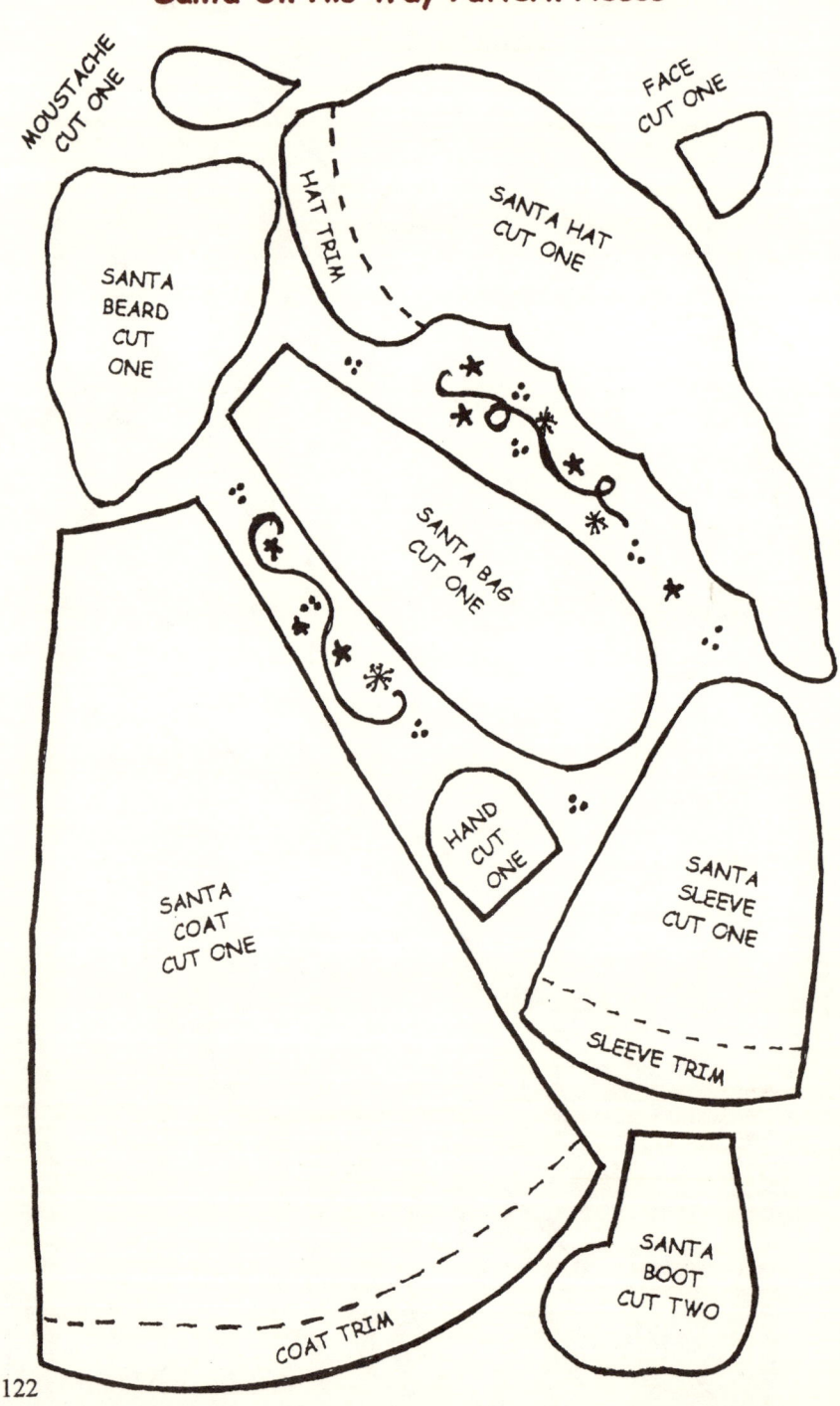

MOUSTACHE CUT ONE

FACE CUT ONE

HAT TRIM

SANTA HAT CUT ONE

SANTA BEARD CUT ONE

SANTA BAG CUT ONE

HAND CUT ONE

SANTA SLEEVE CUT ONE

SANTA COAT CUT ONE

SLEEVE TRIM

SANTA BOOT CUT TWO

COAT TRIM

Santa On His Way
Remaining Pattern Pieces

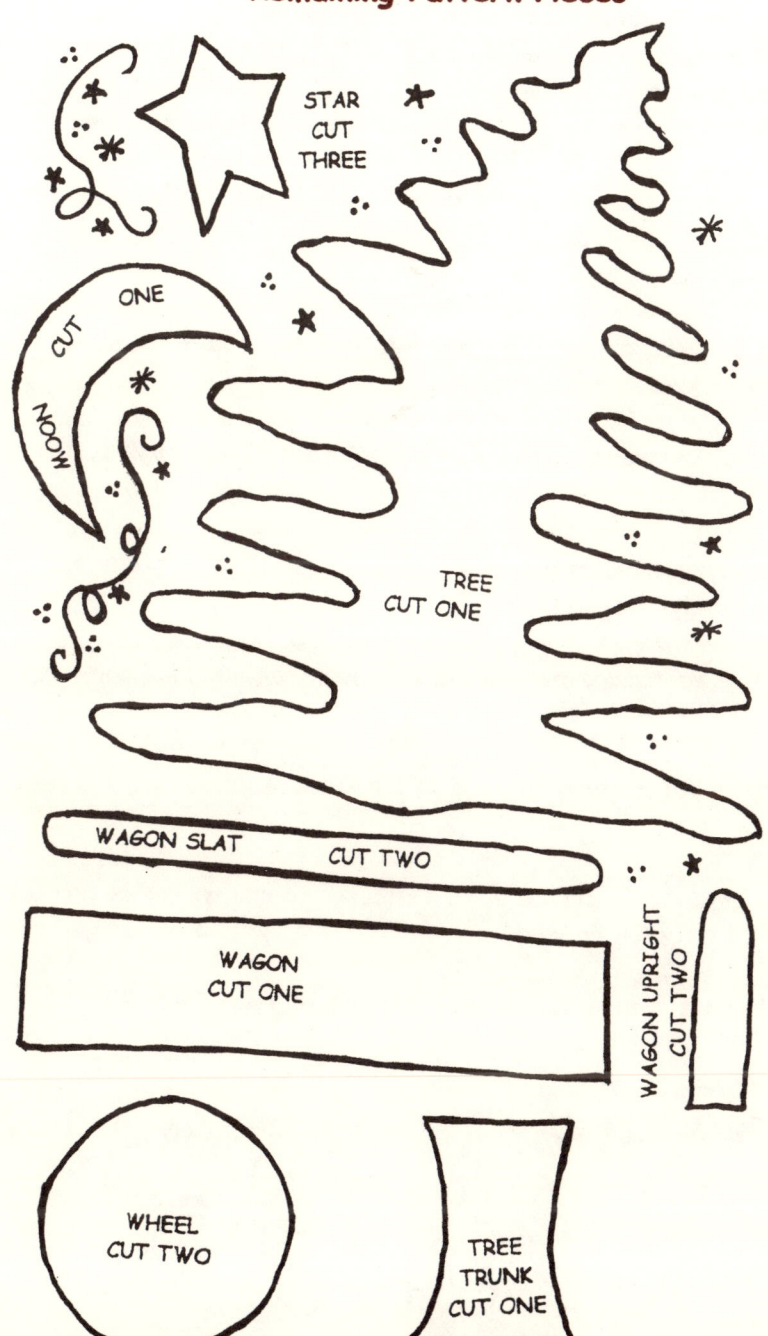

STAR CUT THREE

MOON CUT ONE

TREE CUT ONE

WAGON SLAT CUT TWO

WAGON CUT ONE

WAGON UPRIGHT CUT TWO

WHEEL CUT TWO

TREE TRUNK CUT ONE

Santa On His Way
Instructions:

Make the Double Star Block as instructed on page 16. Trace and cut pattern pieces as stated on each of the patterns shown on the previous pages. Cut each out of "fused" fabric. (See General Instructions on page 4.) Layer "fused" applique fabrics on the star block center. (Refer often to full block drawing for placement ideas.) Iron in place. Blanket stitch around each applique piece. Chain stitch a rope from the wagon to Santa's hand. (See Stitching Instructions on page 6.)

Purchase or make a tree skirt and add this applique around the bottom.

Add several borders to make this block into a festive holiday tablecloth.

Use this applique on brown paper tote bags stuffed with checked tissue for a charming gift bag.

Hang a wall quilt made of this block to make an outside door charmer.

Trace the small drawing on page 121 to create personal greeting cards.

Add the applique described in this chapter to any wearable such as a sweatshirt, apron or vest.

Have a Wonderful Holiday Season All Year Through!

Home Warming Holidays Quilt
72" X 96"

125

Home Warming Holidays Quilt
72" X 96"
Materials Needed and Instructions:

Materials Needed to make entire quilt:
3 yds. Dark Fabric (Star Points and Corner Stones)
3 1/2 yds. Medium Fabric (Background)
1/2 yd. Light Fabric (Center Squares)
1 1/2 yd. Lattice Fabric
1 1/2 yd. Border Fabric
6 yds. Backing Fabric
Queen Size Batting
3/4 yd. Binding

Cutting Instructions:
Cut and make each block as stated on page 4 and each chapter.
Cut 31-2 1/2" X 18 1/2" fabric strips (Lattice)
Cut 20-2 1/2" squares (Corner Stones)
Cut 9-4 1/2" fabric strips (Border)
Cut 9-2 1/2" fabric strips (Binding)

Instructions: Refer to Full Quilt Drawing on page 125 often. Use 1/4" seams throughout.

Lattice:
Make four rows of three blocks each. Separate each block with a lattice strip. Begin and end each row with a lattice strip. You will use sixteen lattice strips. Sew five sets of lattice strips using three 2 1/2" X 18 1/2" strips and four corner stones per set. Sew a set between each row of three blocks. Sew one set on the top and bottom.

Borders:
Sew two and one half strips together for the side borders. Sew two fabric strips together for the top and bottom borders. Sew the borders to the sides, top and bottom on the quilt.

Quilting:
Layer the batting between the top and back fabrics. Pin and quilt. Sew binding strips together. Fold wrong sides together lengthwise. Press. Pin the raw edges of binding around the entire quilt. Sew in place. Trim. Turn the binding to the back of the quilt and slip stitch in place.

Index:

Appetizers:
Apple Cheese Ball	96
Artichoke Dip	96
Cajun Spiced Pecans	99
Dippy Dip	37
Green Chili Sauce	77
Halloween Pate	98
Heavenly Veggies	37
Miracle Dip	37
Mustard Dip	97
Pickled Eggs	36
Seasoned Oyster Crackers	98
Spooky Party Scramble	99
Sunflower Cheese Ball	97
Valley Crackers	36

Beverages:
Champagne Cranberry Punch	20
Egg Nog Punch	120
Irish Crème	30
Labor Day Punch	90
Old Fashioned Lemonade	80
Simple Slush	80
Sparkling Orange Juice	11
Spiced Cider	100
Spiced Coffee Mix	30
Summer Rum Slush	69

Breads:
Apple Corn Bread	88
Butter Twist Coffee Cake	9
Orange Icing	9
Cranberry Bread	109
Date Nut Bread	109
Garlic Parmesan Rolls	59
Golden Corn Bread	57
Holiday Bread	118
Irish Soda Bread	26
Lemon Tea Muffins	46
Mrs. Mc Gregor's Muffins	39
Quick as a Wink Cinnamon Rolls	8

Breakfast:
Easy Breakfast Bake	12
Eggs Extravaganza	12

Cakes/ Pies:
Creamy Carrot Cake	40
Cream Cheese Icing	40
King's Cake	60
Pilgrim Pecan Pie	110
Pumpkin Surprise Pie	110
Satin Slipper Pie	49
Surprise Pie	90
Zucchini Cake	89

Candies:
Caramel Fondue	100
Divine Divinity	120
Festive Fudge	119

Cookies/Bars:
Applesauce Bars	89
Daddy's Oatmeal Cookies	60
Melt My Heart	21
Mint Brownies	29
Snowball Cookies	10
Summer Scrumptious Bars	70
Turtle Cookies	70
Vanilla Wafers	50
White Chocolate Chunk	21

Desserts:
Apple Tortilla	79
Bread Pudding	119
Cheese Cake Bits	49
Chocolate Dream Dessert	20
Glazed Fruit Pizza	48
Irish Crème Dessert	29
Lime Delight	79
Strawberry Surprise	50

Index Continued:

Main Dishes:
Chicken Bake	87
Chicken Grill	67
Corned Beef Casserole	28
Divine Chicken Divan	47
Family Fabulous Turkey	106
Seasoned Stuffing	106
Grilled Ribs	56
Herb Roasted Salmon	57
Honey Bunny Ham	38
Hot Chicken Salad	46
Luscious Lemon Chicken	47
Meat Loaf Pie	26
Oh Heavenly Ham	116
South of the Border Casserole	76
Stove Top Enchilada	77

Salads:
Black Bean Salad	78
Broccoli Salad	27
Caramel Apple Crunch Salad	86
Cottage Potato Salad	58
Cranberry Crunch Salad	108
Frosted Fruit Salad	68
Frozen Champagne Salad	69
Fruity Crunch Salad	11
Little Italy Salad	48
Orange Pineapple Salad	39
Pasta Salad	87
Rainbow Salad	118
Red Raspberry Salad	19
Seven Layer Salad	108
Shrimp Salad	86
Spaghetti Supreme Salad	58
Sunflower Salad	78
Summer Salad	68

Sandwiches:
Regal Reuben	28
Summer Sloppy Joes	66
Summer Submarine	66
Tea Sandwiches	18
Chicken Pineapple Almond	18
Cucumber	18

Vegetables:
Black Hills Baked Beans	56
Carrot Casserole	39
Creole Green Beans	59
Easy Guacamole	76
Family Hash Browns	88
Patch Potatoes	38
Pilgrim Potatoes	107
Quick Potato Soup	27
Red Cabbage and Apples	117
Seasonal Scalloped Corn	116
Summer Slices	67
Twice Baked Potato Casserole	117
Veggie Medley	107

PLEASE SEND ME:

_____ copies of HOME WARMING HOLIDAYS
                COOKBOOK & QUILT PATTERNS @ $19.95 each $ _____
                Tennessee residents add sales tax @ $ 1.75 each $ _____
                Add shipping & handling @ $ 4.50 each $ _____
                Total enclosed $ _____

Mail cookbook(s) to:
Name _____
Address _____
City _____ State _____ Zip _____
            MAKE CHECKS PAYABLE TO STARR★TOOF.
Charge to   ☐ Visa   ☐ MasterCard   Valid thru _____
Account Number_____ Signature _____
Mail to: Toof Cookbooks, Starr★Toof, 670 South Cooper Street, Memphis, TN 38104

PLEASE SEND ME:

_____ copies of HOME WARMING HOLIDAYS
                COOKBOOK & QUILT PATTERNS @ $19.95 each $ _____
                Tennessee residents add sales tax @ $ 1.75 each $ _____
                Add shipping & handling @ $ 4.50 each $ _____
                Total enclosed $ _____

Mail cookbook(s) to:
Name _____
Address _____
City _____ State _____ Zip _____
            MAKE CHECKS PAYABLE TO STARR★TOOF.
Charge to   ☐ Visa   ☐ MasterCard   Valid thru _____
Account Number_____ Signature _____
Mail to: Toof Cookbooks, Starr★Toof, 670 South Cooper Street, Memphis, TN 38104

PLEASE SEND ME:

_____ copies of HOME WARMING HOLIDAYS
                COOKBOOK & QUILT PATTERNS @ $19.95 each $ _____
                Tennessee residents add sales tax @ $ 1.75 each $ _____
                Add shipping & handling @ $ 4.50 each $ _____
                Total enclosed $ _____

Mail cookbook(s) to:
Name _____
Address _____
City _____ State _____ Zip _____
            MAKE CHECKS PAYABLE TO STARR★TOOF.
Charge to   ☐ Visa   ☐ MasterCard   Valid thru _____
Account Number_____ Signature _____
Mail to: Toof Cookbooks, Starr★Toof, 670 South Cooper Street, Memphis, TN 38104

Where did you hear about this cookbook? _____

_____

What local stores would you like to see carry HOME WARMING HOLIDAYS?

_____

Store Name _____ Phone #_____

Address _____

City_____ State _____ Zip _____

Was this cookbook purchased as a gift? _____

What attracted you to this particular cookbook?_____

What is your age? _____

        Thank you in advance for your time and assistance.

Where did you hear about this cookbook? _____

_____

What local stores would you like to see carry HOME WARMING HOLIDAYS?

_____

Store Name _____ Phone #_____

Address _____

City_____ State _____ Zip _____

Was this cookbook purchased as a gift? _____

What attracted you to this particular cookbook?_____

What is your age? _____

        Thank you in advance for your time and assistance.

Where did you hear about this cookbook? _____

_____

What local stores would you like to see carry HOME WARMING HOLIDAYS?

_____

Store Name _____ Phone #_____

Address _____

City_____ State _____ Zip _____

Was this cookbook purchased as a gift? _____

What attracted you to this particular cookbook?_____

What is your age? _____

        Thank you in advance for your time and assistance.